BODY STORY

BODY STORY

Julia K. De Pree

Swallow Press / Ohio University Press

ATHENS

Ohio University Press, Athens, Ohio 45701
© 2004 by Julia K. De Pree

Printed in the United States of America
All rights reserved

Ohio University Press books are printed on acid-free paper ⊗ ™

12 11 10 09 08 07 06 05 04   5 4 3 2 1

Library of Congress Cataloging-in-Publication Data
De Pree, Julia Knowlton.
  Body story / Julia K. De Pree.
     p. cm.
  ISBN 0-8040-1063-3 (alk. paper) — ISBN 0-8040-1064-1 (pbk. : alk.
paper)
  1. De Pree, Julia Knowlton. 2. Anorexia—Patients—United
States—Biography. I. Title.
RC552.A5 D43 2004
362.196'85262'0092—dc22

                                        2003027357

for my daughters

Claire Marguerite and Madeleine Marie

CONTENTS

ACKNOWLEDGMENTS

I would like to extend grateful acknowledgment to those people who encouraged and supported me in the writing of this book:

To my colleagues and students at Agnes Scott College, for their assistance and encouragement: Lerita Coleman Brown, Rosemary Eberiel, Beth Hackett, Waqas Khwaja, Rosemary Lévy-Zumwalt, Marialanna Lee, Michael Lynn, Kelsey McCune, Marylou Menezes, Kristin Miller, Gisela Norat, Rafael Ocasio, Donna Sadler, Amy Whitworth, and Ingrid Wieshofer.

To Nancy Basmajian, for her clarity.

To Gillian Berchowitz, for responding.

To David Sanders, for his gifts of commitment and insight.

To close friends who kept me going: Robin Bellinson and Debby Miller.

And to members of my family, most particularly my husband, Christopher, and my two daughters, for their unfailing devotion.

BODY STORY

1 BODY STORY

This story is not a historical account or a clinical treatise or an impartial narrative. It is a story of one body—mine—in times of illness and creation, and in the disconcerting space of prolonged recovery in between.

The figures within these pages are those of a young girl, a virgin, an anorectic. A writer, a bride, a teacher, a mother.

All of these figures combine now in the voice of this writing. They recede and fade, then emerge to be heard. The light of recollection refracts through a prism of words. The voice of this writing goes into light, then into shadow.

This is the tale of my body in forms of absence and forms of birth, suffering in division and surviving in redemption. My body residing in an interim space between crisis and peace.

I have lived a bodily space of pure absence, of nothingness, of utter loss. This space—starvation—thrust me into a place of death. I am moving ever farther from that space, but its shadow still circles me.

I lived my own disappearance. I felt the harmony of my structure of bone. My flesh became the physical echo of its own existence. Many years have passed since that time. Now my mind is able to tell this story.

What caused my anorexia? What provoked the illness? There are many stories but no clear explanations. I learned growing up that the honorable response to illness was courage—courage proven by silence. My maternal grand-mother was an invalid who could not even speak or turn over in bed on her own. Rheumatoid arthritis had rav-aged her body to the extent that she did not even have the dignity of speech. My father told me my gray-blue eyes came from her. Her face was pretty and I imagined that her voice once had been too.

Her body was so bent and swollen as to be formless underneath her cotton gown with its row of snaps. But, as I remember being told, "she never once complained." When I became ill I vowed to be strong like her. Not complain.

As a child I accepted and internalized a certain sto-icism about physical and emotional suffering. Perhaps it was my English and Scandinavian ancestry that fed this re-sponse. Self-contained, reserved, emotion kept inside. The Midwest with its snow and white birches standing apart. An ice-covered lake, a path of stone. A spare landscape to match restrained emotion.

My anorexia became, simultaneously, a manifestation of silent restraint and a message about its danger. In this story I am attempting to create a memory of presence—a kind of discourse in the place of silence.

Perhaps more significant was the impact of culture in the development of my disorder. I accepted the cultural message that I read in magazines and saw on television as a child. No one helped me resist the dangerous lie at the heart of this message—"a woman's appearance determines her self-worth"—and I could not resist it on my own.

During the month of April 1979, when I was thirteen, both of my grandmothers died. During my final interaction with my father's mother, she reached out a dying hand and playfully fondled my budding breasts. I remember the age spots, liver colored, and the paper quality of her skin. She had dementia at that moment and was not responsible for her actions. Still, I was devastated. I remember what I was wearing: an orange terrycloth tank top with no training bra. I felt enormous shame and confusion about her intrusion. Was something wrong with me? Something in me felt deeply not okay.

This moment of confusion may have been one cause of my consequent starvation. But there is no isolated marker that predated my struggle. Rather, a kaleidoscopic picture. My parents had high standards for me and I held myself to them. Perfectionism, transferred to the female body, meant being thin. I was the middle sister of three and sometimes felt effaced—not the first-born, whom I worshipped, nor the baby, whom I loved and envied. (Her pale curls the color of tassels on ears of corn.) My parents assumed I was okay from all of the outward signs—straight As, musical achievement, shy smiles in my school photos each year. There was no reason for them to be alarmed. They did not know that I was lonely, that I was wasting away. I hid from them.

My sister went away to university and I grieved her absence, not knowing how to be the eldest at home, lost without the protection of her presence.

Regret, but not anger. The need to expose here only that which I can bear.

I did not receive treatment during the most acute phase of my anorexia, as a high school student in Ohio (1983–84). It was a cold spring. I remember tentative lilacs suspended above snow. At five feet ten inches, my weight dipped as low as 114 pounds. My period disappeared along with my breasts and hips—signs of womanhood effaced by the compulsion to starve. The body in disarray, the mind seeking to know the limit of physical form.

My desire to fold myself into pure absence was the desire to know the center of my being. I sought in absolute silence and physical stasis a kind of communication beyond ordered meaning. It was like passing through a silver mirror to the other side in pure light.

It was dizzying, blinding. I had conquered my body's physical needs, its messy demands. Yet in return I had relegated myself to a most remote place in my mind where all understanding had come undone. That center was a point of nonbeing.

I could not remain in this state of disorder. The imperative of everyday living pulled me back to its details, its meaning and order. This story describes a fall into pure disappearance and the slow return to the vulnerability of living.

There are aspects of this insidious illness that have never left me, may not ever leave. I have learned to understand some of this. A loneliness, very quiet. Hush of light passing through leaves. A quality of observation and partial participation. A confrontation with the ambivalence of the body's needs. A daily struggle with all forms of my hunger—hunger for food, for understanding, for the body's desires.

Now in this story I open my deepest hunger—the desire to be heard and to be understood. For this communication I have long been famished. I feel less lonely writing this to you.

The silent spaces interspersed in this writing echo the remote places in my mind, the inscription of my solitude, its blind center. These blank spaces also speak the rhythm of your breathing and the rhythm of my breathing.

My anorexia was a bridge of absence, leading me from innocence to experience, from girlhood to womanhood. My hunger was a virgin space, blank passion, moving me in circles further and further within. Leading me to the knowledge of my own uncertainty.

I fought my way back from starvation during that cold spring. I was seventeen. I renounced my own invisibility in order to move tentatively toward the presence of this meaning, communication of my longing.

Contemporary American culture celebrates and effectively prescribes starvation as a physical ideal. It is not surprising, then, that complete recovery often proves to be elusive.

The chronic qualities of anorexia have felt at times like hail pelting a square pane of glass, the tide beating the shore, pausing in respite only to resume. Sometimes I relapse, or begin to relapse. I catch myself falling and pick myself up again.

This body story will go to places of living that occur in between order and disorder—my knowledge alternating with the doubt of instability. Is that in-between state of open vulnerability not the true space of reality?

The vulnerability of creating a new life that will die, of the ache of desire here in present memory, of writing a story that confronts the uncertain hold of reality.

I monitor the physical indications of my recovery: a body weight within a "normal" range for my height, a medically acceptable percentage of body fat, bright red blood that flows regularly each month.

Blood and milk reveal my return to life, tell a new story. My body survived the self-imposed starvation and has twice resided in the garden of birth. Garden of flesh, of warmth, of movement. Round belly of life, heavy breasts, my two daughters—halos of wet hair crowning as they leave the dark home of my womb. My body opening outward in circles and tearing in the act of giving birth.

Some seventeen years after my darkest starvation, I found the treatment that I needed so badly. The daily pill in the shape of an ellipse. Zoloft, one hundred milligrams. The fifty-milligram pill blue, the hundred-milligram pill a pale yellow.

More important than medication is language. Telling the story. I have consulted with seven or eight psychotherapists/psychiatrists since the age of eighteen. Trial and error. Two spoke only about themselves. One told me what I needed was a new outfit. Another came close to being right but then she became pregnant and went away. Number seven teased me when I described stomach upset from the antidepressant. White coat and stethoscope. Brown eyes. His teasing was a veiled form of flirtation. Flirting was not what I needed. I was so desperate to speak that I was losing my way within the nonliving state of depression—its cruel monotony, the open stare of its fitful sleep. By this time I was an assistant professor of French and was married with two very young daughters.

On a dark, chill evening in November 1999, I finally found the psychiatrist who would be willing to go with me into the story of my starvation, to attempt to decipher the enigma of experience—first the physical and emotional experience, then the fifteen-year fallout from the lack of treatment.

This psychiatrist has been the first to listen to my story. First in fragments, then in coherent pieces, pictures form-

6

ing within my words. I lie on the couch in his office and try to tell my story: the story of disappearing evolving into the story of being, of teaching and of knowing, of writing this story.

His attention and care have brought me back to my body and to the vulnerability of my voice. He is not afraid of my uncertainty, the ever-present possibility of relapse. He accepts the hunger of these words.

My speech falters and flows. I am attuned to the scratch and the quiet of his pen, to the manner in which he shifts his weight in his chair. His voice is the point of orientation for my longing.

Because I lie down I am deprived of visual communication, the satisfactions of the gaze. Nevertheless there are two coordinates in my peripheral vision upon which I rely to see his presence: a vague outline of his face in my right field of vision, the black tip of his shoe when I turn on my left side.

Alone in the presence of the other. Speaking myself back to understanding. After so many wrong turns and false starts—this is the voice, this is the presence.

He meets my gaze when I enter his office and again when I leave. I often cannot look into his eyes but not once has he looked away.

If I arrive in the morning, I regard the straight vacuumed lines on his carpet while lying on the couch. Straight lines in opposition to the associations of my words, the circle of stones in what remains unsaid. I wonder about the employee who vacuums his carpet. Who she is and what she thinks as she pushes the noisy machine in even rows across his office floor. The little yellow light on the front of the vacuum.

This Christmas I come close to relapse. Stress of the holidays. My weight dips too low, beneath the normal minimal range for my height. I catch myself. I tell him about it. I say things I wanted to describe when I was seventeen but could not. I tell part of the story you are holding in your hands.

2 GIRL BODY

Born in Cleveland, Ohio, in the bitter January cold. Winter baby. 1966. My mother's body completely anesthetized while it pushed me out. Within twenty-four hours, her breasts were bound tight so that I could not nurse.

I write this and it is true.

She sat on her hospital bed while registered nurses wound flat pieces of fabric tightly around her chest. She spent the next two nights in pain from the tension of life milk being cut short and held back. I slept in my hospital bassinet. Newborn body with slate-gray eyes. Seven and a half pounds.

I know that I think about this more than I should. Yet something within me cannot shake these depths of regret. I try to understand it and I cannot. From the beginning, some urge was starved—the tiny body reaching out, the fundament of need unrequited.

This baby grows and becomes a girl, embodied innocence with no knowledge of desire's aggressions, wholeness unbroken, unimagined, unknown.

I remember the feel of the body of a girl—lightness of step, light to the touch, running, skipping, pure movement, pure form. I remember jumping into the same lake ten thousand times and skating every winter on the same thick frozen pond. The body of a girl is a bird, a lantern—made of teardrops, teacups, musical notes. It is mobility and grace and it never fails.

My girl body acted as a subject in the world. I was fortunate to have lived that bodily subject. So many little girls immediately become objects on a stage of physical desire, their subjectivity reduced to a theatrical illusion.

I was lucky. I felt good in my girl's body—its little windmill of legs and arms, its speed, its dance, its turning in circles. I remember how the grass looked while I did handstands, the hot scratch of sand on my welcoming skin.

Do you remember the time before your body ached within its own provocations, before you realized that it was culturally for sale, literally up for grabs, before you began to notice its being taken away from you?

To be truly in a girl's body is not to be aware of one's physical virginity. The virgin body is aware of its actual integrity; and being aware, it cannot take it for granted. The girl's body is different: it is not yet aware and thus is purer than pure.

The girl looks at women's bodies—her mother's, her teacher's, her aunts', their friends'—and imagines them merely as a further wholeness, like innocence matured. The inevitable suffering of assumed passivity blissfully does not occur to her. This is the true virginity. The virgin is merely waiting—at times impatiently, at times reluctantly—to survive desire's game.

The virgin body knows exactly what it's getting into.

My girl body was good at hide and seek, sliding its slim form under beds, behind drawers and cornered stairs. Innocence allows the body the fun of hide and seek. Later, in the throes of my starving body, I went into a frightening hiding place and was almost never found. I was trying—hard—to escape the cultural prescription of bodily passivity by disappearing silently into physical eclipse.

I try to maintain this writing of my physical innocence, but it was such a brief time that it slips away from these words. There was swimming and there were long walks in the woods. There was homemade blueberry pie and there were bluegill fish caught and strung on a hook. If the fish was too small my dad would throw it back. One tiny splash and it was gone. I remember watching it swim away, wondering how it would fare after being hooked and handled in the air.

I used to watch the light move in the poplars and birches in the summer, in northern Michigan where my family stayed. In late summer in the evenings before the northern lights, that light was sublime and without end.

In my girl's body, I thought I would always comprehend the path of that light. I never thought I would lose myself to shadow along the way.

I felt like the light filtered in among the thousand leaves. I never thought my physical form would be forsaken. Nor did I imagine what creation it might bring forth.

I watch my daughters now as their bodies move in that girlhood bliss. They are graceful and strong and they do not fail. The elder jumps fearlessly off diving boards, climbs high, and pirouettes. My toddler runs and jumps and is learning how to skip. The ground is still close enough to prevent harm when she falls.

My daughters' bodies bring me back to my own. The girl's body inhabits its own grace and transparency, which is its own language. I miss this so much: that state of nature before the intrusions of culture.

I remember the natural ebb and flow of waking and sleep cradling me in that finite girlhood life. Too soon, its gentleness was broken. My first bout with insomnia began at age eight. Already, my mind and imagination's fear were conspiring against my physical peace.

My mother's absence provoked my struggle to sleep. She was attending night classes. My whole body would lie there, awake and still, thoroughly longing for her return. *If I fall asleep she may never come back, I may never see her again, I will keep watch in my small bed in the night.*

Taking a break from this writing, I walk outside into eight inches of rare Atlanta snow. I travel eight loops around the same cold track, my black coat with no buttons billowing in the wind like some wild, grounded bird. At my first turn around, I see the form of an angel traced in the snow. Thinking of the body I once had as a girl, I remember all the lively angels my fluttering arms and legs once made.

I could never get enough of them. Over the years, I must have left an entire heavenly host to crust with ice and melt in the northern Ohio snows.

Upon walking farther, I see another imprint on the track: huge letters made of footprints that form the words "F-U-C-K M-E." In an instant the angel memory disappears, replaced by the connotations of this crude, earthly imperative.

I wish I could have turned into one of my angels, a picture in the snow. Fleeting and pristine, a perfect absence so divinely *not there*.

Surely the angel I saw today and its profane accompanying snow-text point to the contrast in this part of my body story: the angel telling and remembering the sheer delight of its movement, the words a static violation of the snow's clean form.

The angel is the message proclaimed by every girl body: transcendent, pristine, beyond desire's failures or memory's broken reach.

Those footprint-words that I read in the snow are the message proclaimed—unwittingly—by every virgin body: fragmented, imperfect, possessed by passion in its futile clutch.

I remember my girl's body as a source of self-knowledge. I heard in it its own language, the words of my existence and daylight's song. Through it, I measured the world's spaces and hidden forms. I knew the size of a tree by how long it took to climb it, the weight of a stone by its heft in my hand.

Mostly, I did not struggle to perceive myself. Now self-perception is something I cannot escape. It was wonderful merely to be in the world without seeing in the world a mirror into which to peer. The innocence of the girl body faded too fast.

My starvation was my resistance to leaving this realm. I resisted for several years by effacing my body's physical signs of sexuality: hips, breasts, cycle of blood.

The starving body is a body in protest. Anorexia is a hunger strike against the cultural injustice of the female body-commodity. The anorectic is saying—through her body—that her body is not ready to confront the agency of desire. Her form is the physical expression of her reluctance, her fear, all that she cannot say.

A girl's innocence is like light through the leaves, a picture traced in snow—a slight beauty that moves, elusive in its wholeness, its self-knowledge, its center of grace.

I remember trusting my body and its language of reverence. It led and I followed. I went forward and it drew near.

Was it not wonderful to know the answers to your body's questions, before the doubt set in? Was it not lovely to trust the limits of desire, desire's maze, the danger and the price of loving and being loved in return? The child's body is a body to have and to hold, without the need for any vow.

I remember swimming for hours on end, my skin turning brown "as a nut," as my father used to say. Northern water and light baptized my skin, warming and illuminating birch and stone.

I recall bicycles, roller skates, skateboards, all wheeling me toward the next place of my knowing, the next stretch of sidewalk waiting for my glide. I flew down frozen hills on a wooden sled or plastic saucer—no one could ever catch me, I was so free. My slight body was pure motion in white snow. Skating swiftly across thick, silver ice, nothing existed beyond the sound of the blade on that frozenness, the movement of my warm body through frigid air.

By the time I was twelve or thirteen, the skating had become a social ritual for boys and girls to meet. My best friend and I would wonder together, as we listened to each song being piped onto the rink, who might ask us for a boy-girl skate, and when, and for how long.

In that brief dream body there was no pain. Perhaps I can reach back to it now, here in memory's words.

I know that girl is playing somewhere in this garden. She may be skipping stones or she may be dozing in the sun. Perhaps it is twilight and she is playing hide and seek. I see her darting among the birches and in between these shadows.

The white of the birches stands out against the dark.

If I could find this little girl again I would not disturb her play.

I would not trespass her earthly grace, the perfect form for which there are no words—

Only this quietness and a sweet adieu.

Memory circling back again.

I am eight years old. Cleveland, Ohio. 1974. I have been fed. I have been bathed. It is time for reading. Outside it is dark and it is cold. Was my father still at work?

My mother is reading to me and to my two sisters. I am in the middle, the quiet, blue-eyed one. I have long arms and legs, I am slight and innocent, I am a very young girl. My hair is golden dark and cropped. My father is not there. The TV is on at the foot of my parents' bed. I am curled against my mother's left side.

There is snow outside, snow falling in rhythms like the passing images on the TV. My attention alternates between the words on the page, the sound of my mother's voice, and the grown-up movie that is being shown on the screen.

There is the feel of my mother's warmth, the words she is reciting, and the imperious image of the TV screen. The book she is reading is mild and honest. The movie on the TV is violent and honest. One is innocence, one is experience. I have no recollection of the book beyond its gentle weight, the sound of the pages being turned. What I remember is the televised narrative, held forth, flaunted, haunting me even to this day.

I know that this was a kind of primal scene.

The movie, Born Innocent, depicted the prison life of female delinquents, so-called bad girls. I have no idea why it was on, but my mother was watching it as she read to us.

I was watching too. A new inmate was admitted. A petite, brown-haired teenage girl. The characters on the screen are rough and wild, yelling and smoking and swearing at each other. My mother is reading. Her body is pure warmth. Outside the Midwest is blank and cold.

Now something is happening on the screen but I do not know what. The new girl at this institution for delinquents was trying to fit in, but she kept getting excluded. She is in the communal bathroom. The girl steps out of the shower. The others are standing in a half circle around her. Instead of a towel for her, they are carrying a broom with the straw side down. Pointing toward her is the wooden broomstick.

They grab her and pull her down to the floor, naked and wet. She screams and resists but there are four or five of them pressing her to the floor. I am eight years old and I am watching this.

I protest to my mother: "Mommy, look what they are doing!"

She knows what they are doing but she does not want to think that I know. The movie stays on. My mother tells me to pay attention to the book. My older sister is there;

I do not know if she is watching. My baby sister is already in bed.

The storybook and my mother's warmth.

The television and its cold fear.

I try to pay attention to the bedtime rhyme but I cannot. I look at my mother's face and watch her gaze directed above the top of the children's book, looking at the TV screen. It must have been one of those books that children demand to have recited again and again. My mother's mouth recited the story while I watched her watch the scene on TV.

The new inmate has her hands and feet held down. Another one covers her mouth so that the warden won't hear her screams. My mind takes in forever the meaning of the victim's silence.

The broomstick disappears halfway up in between the victim's legs. Then it comes out again. The girl writhes and twists, her muffled screams covered by an unknown hand. Repetition again. The broomstick thrust in and removed, violating her, hurting her again and again.

Thrust. The broomstick shoved in and pulled out. The tile bathroom floor. The row of white sinks.

The perpetrators decide the initiation has lasted long enough. They let go of the victims' arms and legs and uncover her mouth. She is defeated. A faucet is on; water is flowing into the sink without anyone standing in front of it. There is blood. I am eight.

The other women drop the broom beside the victim and file silently away.

I wish I could have forgotten all about this but I could not. These images instilled my fright about growing from a girl into a woman. On that winter night, a fear grew in me about the violence surrounding a woman's body, its authority, its weakness.

I don't know why that movie was projected into my parents' room on that night. Perhaps it does not matter anymore. Why was I exposed to something so violent as a child?

This is a question for which there is no answer. And if there were, it would make no sense. What matters is that my mind has gripped this for so long. There is only the memory of what I saw in combination with the bedtime book and my mother's soft warmth. Something in me became afflicted that night. Some conflict, knot of tension, arose deep inside my child's mind. In some way I put myself in the victim's place. In some way I had been violated. I tried to pay attention only to the colorful book with its oversized pages. Instead I had absorbed another story, a story about power and sex and authority and might. It made me very afraid to become a woman. I wanted to remain nestled against my mother, with the storybook, without the TV story.

Something in this memory has provoked this body story.

I can still see the victim lying alone on the tile floor. She had passed the initiation, being raped with a broomstick. She would become one of them. Her passage from ignorance to experience has been claimed. Would she then repeat the injustice with the next initiate who would come to their group?

Something in my eight-year-old mind decided I had better avoid being hurt like that. Even if it meant that I must remain a girl.

Something in my eight-year-old heart did not know how I could.

My mother tucked me in. I lay still with my soft doll or teddy bear. The panes of the windows were etched with ice. The curtains sewn by my mother dropped a veil between my room and the bitter night. I closed my girl eyes, the lashes touching my cheeks. I fell asleep without thinking of anything. Nothing at all.

Now, almost thirty years later, I recall this memory of violation, of broken trust, of the snow falling outside, the family's Siamese cat taking it all in with his cool blue eyes. My wild astonished fear.

3 VIRGIN BODY

I am fifteen. It is warm and green in Ohio. My girlfriends and I have been socializing with a group of boys who attend private school. They drive and have money and they have found us out.

My mother buys me a white dress at a shop called My Darling Daughter, a boutique where she would normally never go. It is the nicest dress she has ever bought for me. It has spaghetti straps and lace trim and a matching jacket. I feel pretty when I try it on. My mother frowns as she looks at the handwritten price tag but she agrees to buy it.

It will be another two years before the anorexia takes hold. At fifteen, I have had my period only once or twice. I am naturally tall and slim. I know nothing and my body is just emerging from the marvelous innocence of girlhood with its long afternoons and clean sheets, its stockings filled with toys.

I have photos from this formal date. A photo of me standing alone in the backyard shows the pale blue ribbon I had tied around my waist. I had matched it to a pale blue purse. Another photo shows me standing with my date. My father had faithfully documented the moment.

I remember the backyard as I posed in that white dress. To the left was the apple tree and to the right was the pear tree. Neither was able to bear edible fruit. The tight little domes that dropped from the tree's branches merely turned the lawn into a minefield for my dad's mower. My sisters and I were required to gather and dispose of the plentiful, bitter fruit.

But the lawn was soft and green. I see my white ballerina slippers edged in blades of grass. It must have been June.

I remember almost nothing of the actual dance. The boys took their dates quickly away, to the home of one boy whose parents were out of town. I remember the party's host, a very tall, broad-shouldered, wealthy teenage boy.

I remember a game room and a house fancier than I had ever seen before. In the game room was a pool table and a dartboard and a bar. There were kegs of beer. I remember having one glass.

The next thing I recall is being out in the van with my date. He was on top of me in a literal spasm of desperate, adolescent male desire. I was one small step removed from his usual masturbation, a warm object covered in that lace-trimmed dress.

The boy had nothing to say—no words, no asking, and no reply. I tried to move out from under him but he persisted. I kept pushing him away until I managed to be free.

That is all I remember from that night. I do not know how I got home. I must have returned home with the other girls but I do not remember. I did not tell anyone about what happened. My parents must have asked me about the evening and I must have told them it was fine.

Last summer my six-year-old daughter ran into the house crying about an incident that happened while she was playing with a neighborhood boy. He had pinned her beneath him and, in her words, "wouldn't get off me."

The boy's parents scolded him for playing too forcefully.

I want to protect her forever and I cannot.

As my body moved me into young womanhood, my own feelings were becoming lost to me. My body's girl language that I had come to know and to trust was slowly being translated into new terms. The new language was the adult language in which the body becomes the object of passionate desire.

I could no longer reach my body's authenticity and integrity. Something had been stolen from within. Did I forsake my body like a house mindlessly left open? The end seemed to happen so fast.

Had I left that girl's garden, or had it forsaken me?

Ages fifteen through seventeen. There were other boys, more dates, other special dresses bought in anticipation. I entered high school and dated a senior who came looking my way. He was a few inches shorter then I was and used to stand on a stack of books at our lockers to tease me about my height. He was kind and sweet and he reached that elusive third base with me over and over again. I remember his basement with the couch and the TV, his parents' approving smiles, their plastic tumblers of ice cubes and Coke.

My girlfriends and I went out to parties with this group of boys two years older. There was a lot of drinking; I remember vodka and cranberry juice, vodka and orange juice. Outside, black winter limbs and bitter snow, a disc of moon. Ice cubes in transparent glasses, the silver transparence of the vodka. The boys, grinning and shining their bright eyes, complimented themselves on their ability to mix drinks.

I remember a boy, another senior, who became preoccupied by his desire for me, but I refused to go on a date with him. I remember the heat in his insistent stare and I vaguely see his face now as I write these words.

I had no sense of what I was doing. I remember that I did like making out with the boyfriend who was shorter than I was. I did care about him and he made me feel safe.

High school boys knew how to talk to me, how to say nice things and pay compliments and give me valentines.

Most of these boys were tall and lean and sandy-haired. I remember witnessing desire in a lot of blue eyes. This was the Midwest, where people come from Scandinavian ancestry.

One of the only boys to whom I felt deep attraction was black. I danced with him late into the night one night. I wish I could have told him that he made me feel safe.

I was still a child in a virgin body. I had no sense of the depth of my physical desire, no understanding of the feelings provoked by my body and aroused within it.

And something was starting to go very wrong. I was

losing my way in this complicated maze, losing the game of hide and seek.

One of my close friends had a brother at Miami University, located a few hours from Cleveland. She asked me to come with her to visit him and I did, more than once. My friend and I lied to our parents and said we were going to visit classes and go to the football game. Our parents chose to believe this.

My friend and I did go to football games, but instead of classes we were guests of honor at the brother's fraternity parties. Sweet sixteen. We even slept in the brother's room in the fraternity house.

My parents put me on a bus with my friend more than once to allow me this exposure to college life. It is not for me now to wonder why: I was almost a straight-A student and I was a good liar.

I remember one college boy in the fraternity, that same gaze of heat with which he looked at me. The heat of wanting to enter inside. I danced with him. He was tall and held me close. He told me he knew I was very young. My friend's older brother kept his peers from violating my friend and me. He made sure his friends knew how young we were and what grade we were in.

One time a group from the fraternity house took off on a road trip in the middle of the night. My friend and I went. We rode in the backs of cars in the black night into another state and arrived at the same fraternity at Indiana U. I was sixteen and traveling with a fraternity, in another state without my parents' knowledge.

I remember being up all night. So many college boys with their bright eyes and seductive, college-boy smiles.

I was in way over my head. I had just enough sense not to end up raped—no more, no less.

I knew what was happening in those fraternity bedrooms and I did not go in.

And yet all of this experience somehow added up to a slow, symbolic violation, taking me far away from myself and destroying my girl's sense of confidence and trust.

I remember going to the high school senior prom when I was in my junior year. I was seventeen and emaciated, suffering from untreated anorexia nervosa. My date was tall and awkward and hardly knew what to say to me.

Again, my mother bought me a dress. This one was cream colored and floor-length, with a high collar and a wide satin sash. The shoulders and neck were made of tulle netting, and the dress was designed to be worn without a bra. The point was moot since I was too starved even to fill out my first training bra.

A photo from that night shows me all dressed and ready to go. In the photo you can see the sharp lines of my collarbone, as if forming the letter Y in the word *why*.

I had so little flesh on my arms and shoulders that the tulle netting just floated above my body's contours.

Maybe I was turning into one of those snow angels.

All I remember from that prom is dancing with my date. During the slow dances I contemplated—as if my mind were disengaged from the experience—the hot press of his erection searching the gauzy folds of my dress.

The stakes of desire felt very dangerous indeed. To give myself over to desire I felt as if I had to lose myself. I did not know how to speak what I felt, or perhaps I did not know how to feel. I was becoming as remote as a shadow on snow.

I remember all of the hands in this time of my body's virginity. Grasping, groping, the early adolescence of desire a language with absolutely no subtlety and no restraint. The hands of a boy's virgin desire trace their urgent questions on the girl's clothed form. They say the same word every time: *please, please, please, please.*

This virgin touching was a kind of clumsy sport in which the girl stumbles to make up the rules: *here, not there, okay, now stay, now leave, maybe tomorrow, not today.*

What does a boy's virginity mean to him? It seemed to be a physical embarrassment that he was desperate to get beyond. The girl's body was the means to this end. It seemed to me that the boy's physical desire felt to him like a runaway train.

My virginity felt like holding on to the light that I watched passing through the leaves. It meant climbing the branches of the apple tree. It meant cotton tennis shoes and clean tape on my scraped knees. I never wanted it to end.

And yet, the fruit hanging among the leaves of desire was beginning to attract all five of my virgin senses.

I held onto my virginity for a long time. Of the boys who tried in vain to have it, the last one I will recall is a boy I dated at age seventeen. He was a freshman at Cleveland State. I see now that this series of slightly older boys increased my sense of passivity and lack of control. Older boys always look for younger girls.

I met this boy through my older sister's boyfriend. I

can still see his face and remember the details of his hands. His hands were not beautiful and he chewed his nails repeatedly to the quick.

I was totally lost to myself in the months I was dating this boy. I was moving deeper into the anorexia. I would smoke pot while watching TV with him late into the night in his home. I remember him filling the little bowl of his bong, patting the bulbs and weeds firmly into place. I remember putting my mouth to the spout, the awful smell and taste, the bubbles in the water.

We would drink beer and make out. I tried to tell him my fears about my inability to eat. He told me he really didn't understand. He was the only one to whom I tried to describe it.

When he tried to convince me to drop acid with him, I found the strength to shake myself awake from this starving, depressed state. I told him no. He told me that the little paper squares were really colorful and had fun pictures like Mickey Mouse on them. I repeated, *no, no, no*. He tried adamantly to convince me to have sex. I told him *no, I was not ready*.

After enough unsuccessful cajoling he decided not to try any more. After about six months of dating, we went our separate ways.

My parents knew nothing of my dating life. I kept my confusion and my desperation to myself. I was in the top 5 percent of my class. At school I was singing madrigals in a selective choir and I was reading sophisticated literature in French. I was also a serious student of the violin. My teacher was a violinist with the Cleveland Orchestra. I was mastering vibrato and I would rehearse a single concerto for a year. I go back to the music now and it is a dense forest of notes accompanied by my teacher's scrawl. Some of it I can still play; some of it I cannot.

I remember my teacher holding each finger down on the string with his elderly hands. He would move my finger back and forth, back and forth, teaching it physically to vibrate the string. In teaching me, he pressed so hard that my teenage fingers were crisscrossed with deep creases from the string.

Here was a different kind of touch from male hands: intelligent, respectful, disciplined with care. Here was a man who cared about my talent and my mind, about the mastery and interpretation of musical form.

During this time I had an English teacher who I believe also saved me from my self-destruction. He taught me that I might go into language and make there my safety. He taught me about the freedom of words and the virgin integrity of the poem. He showed me that writing could become my boat, sail, and sea.

At the height of my confused, starving virginity, I began to write. The first poem spilled out of me during a kind of delirium of work, music, and hunger. I showed it to my teacher. He called my parents on the phone and asked them to come and talk with him. They came home from the meeting and told me that my teacher thought I had real literary talent. He wanted me to continue to write. My parents were proud.

My virgin body was in a state of disintegration and these teachers were showing me the way back to creation.

As a high school senior, I found my first love. He was my age and took French with me. He used to copy my homework while we ate lunch. He went to Yale and he wanted to marry me. He was gentle and subtle and with him I was not afraid. He respected what my mind could do.

His body reached for mine and my body responded. We went cross-country skiing and drank hot chocolate.

I was in love. I was able to tell him about the fear of my starvation. He soothed me and listened and gave me music and books.

Like the other boys, he too wanted to be inside me. Unlike the boys before him, I was ready to give. I waited until I was eighteen. I got birth control on my own with him by my side.

My parents went out of town, and I agreed.

The first time we made love it did not hurt me at all. And I was surprised that there was no blood. Just him inside.

Of course I did not understand the act, did not derive any real womanly pleasure. It was innocent and sweet and it was spring.

But he was a teenage boy. He had bragged to his friends in secret about our plans for that night. While we slept, they had come into my backyard and toilet-papered the fruit trees. The toilet paper hung in long, tattered ribbons amid the twisted, bitter fruit.

I sat on the back patio in a blue robe and looked at that sight.

I was no longer a virgin and it had not hurt.

4 STARVING BODY

Ohio

In the spring of 1983 I began in earnest to starve myself.
I was just seventeen. There is no single answer to the question why.

Most of the girls in my social group were dieting.
Standing on the risers during choir practice on stage, a
close friend described her test for herself each morning:
was her seventeen-year-old stomach concave when standing upright in the shower? If not, she had eaten too much
the day before.

In the hallway in high school, the rush of books and
lockers. Padlocks opening, locker doors slamming, notebooks and jackets being put in and taken out. There is a set
of twin girls in my year, class of 1984. One of the twins is
severely anorexic. I am fighting my way back from the illness during my senior year. I stand watching the girl: she

is like a tiny bird and could easily fit into her locker with lots of room to spare. She misses weeks of classes at a time because of hospitalization. Her face is a skull with short dark hair. Her healthy twin sister has long hair and a normal body weight, but she seems haunted as well. The afflicted twin could not attend college. I do not know what happened to her.

Another friend in high school existed solely on gum and large diet Cokes. She was terribly, terribly ill. Whatever food she did eat she threw up right away. Her hair was brittle and breaking into pieces, her teeth were mottled from stomach acid, her face was becoming an image of disappearance. The rest of us were sick but she was much sicker. We tried to talk with her—like the blind leading the blind—but she would have none of it.

This social group was white, fairly affluent, and high-achieving—the typical demographic for girls who develop eating disorders. My circumstances for anorexia nervosa read like a case study: it was as if my background had been a prelude to the development of the affliction.

Again, I was lucky. I caught myself before I fell too far. I shook myself awake and something inside me would not let me pass into pure shadow.

This part of my body story is not about statistics or case studies. It is simply an inscription of my starving body, my will to disappear.

I manifested many of the clinical behaviors of the illness: stubborn compulsion, near-total restriction, denial of the physical suffering, hiding tactics, emotional evasion. I wrote down all of my calories at the end of each day, making short lists in a pink journal of everything that passed my lips:

Apple	60
cottage cheese half cup	90
small V-8	45

The illness developed rapidly, in large part because I am naturally slim. There were many days when my total caloric intake did not exceed 600 calories. I weighed myself with great ritual every morning.

Stand on the scale, look, step off. Stand on the scale, look, step off. Stand on the scale, look, step off. Make yourself stop repeating this. Step into the hot shower.

The morning is the time for weighing because the body has slept and it is empty. No shoes, no jeans, no stomach full of food.

My appetite erased itself during the worst time of my illness. This was my body's will to survive. The body adjusts its metabolism to the nearly nonexistent food intake, so as to conserve energy and keep itself alive. I do not remember feeling very hungry as my weight went down to 130, down through the 120s, and down again through the teens.

When I got down to 114 pounds, I was too weak to raise my arms above my head. I remember very clearly standing in front of my bedroom mirror and deciding to lift my leg as in a ballet lift. I did not have the strength.

It was the spring of 1983. The crocuses and a few tulips started to poke through the snow. The lilac tree thrived on the side of the house, near the little door where the milkman used to place glass bottles of milk with foil caps.

The Midwest was returning to life and I was experiencing an encounter with destruction. I was rapidly and willfully wasting away.

Hipbones like the edges of wings. Ribs like a row of bare trees. Collarbones forming that letter Y. Knees and elbows knobby circles of bones.

The tailbone starting to protrude.

At the point when the tailbone begins to stick out, sitting in a hard chair becomes very uncomfortable. A backpack full of heavy books can bang that tailbone and make it hurt.

When the body reduces itself to its structure of bones, it is cold.

The ribs appear. The thin fingers can nestle in between them.

My starving body was a journey to the edge of what it meant to be alive. I lived right at that edge for several months, and it is hard to remember many details. I remember the scale placed under the window in the blue marble bathroom my sister and I had shared. During my starvation she was away at college. I missed her more than I knew how to admit.

I remember the softness of my bed and where it was placed in my room. I clearly remember writing my first poems, and recording the brief lists of my food intake.

For a few days I existed almost entirely on gum and hard candy. At dinner I would have lettuce. My period went away. I was studying harder than I ever had in my life. I would study for seven hours in my room on a Saturday and then practice a concerto on my violin.

In a paradoxical way, I starved my body in order to understand my life. I had to place my body in suspension before I could move physically into my sexuality. Starving allowed me to create an interim space between innocence and experience, between being a girl and being a woman.

My starving body was the edge of my life. I needed to travel that edge, to move along it in circles and in straight lines, to go deep into my mind without the physical form.

I became an empty purity: mercury in a glass thermometer, the edge of a white wing flying in blue space, a drift of clean snow, a white sheet hanging on a line.

I still sometimes miss how that felt: perfectly light, like rain, like a dance. No soft flesh to carry around, no breasts, no buttocks, no round warm weight.

My hands had become fluttering birds, flying over the violin strings and over my French verbs, making their home among books and poems.

I was pure movement in new air, a vocabulary of blue light and white bones. I was a story being told without the anchor of form.

I was reading Shakespeare and John Donne: *death be not proud, the quality of mercy is not strained.* I was reading *Candide* and giving oral reports on it in advanced French. *Le meilleur des mondes possibles:* the best of all possible worlds.

My body had conquered its physical needs. There was no desire unmet because there was no more desire. I read in Voltaire to cultivate one's garden while the garden of my body was slipping into winter.

The starving brain spits out endorphins like natural painkillers. They give the anorectic a kind of high, like a light-headed dizziness to take the pain away. I still feel that sometimes. Apparently the high is addictive.

During the spring of 1983 I was only vaguely aware of my condition. In May, my older sister came home from college and looked at me and became instantly very upset. I remember her asking my parents urgently to look at me, to look at my weight. *"Look at her, look at her!"* I had been hiding my body in oversized clothes and my feelings were buried inside of my bones.

My sister brought attention to my illness. I was taken to the pediatrician by my mother. I remember sitting lightly on the examination table, a paper doll in a paper dress. The pediatrician looked at the history of my weight loss and calmly diagnosed a case of borderline anorexia.

I think now that his diagnosis was wrong. At 114 pounds, I was significantly underweight. I was not menstruating. I was weak and depressed and denied my condition. I believe this misdiagnosis prolonged the illness. Because I was diagnosed with a "borderline" eating disorder, my parents and I were able to look the other way.

My mother took me to her gynecologist. I had my first pelvic exam. I was still a virgin. I was given five days' worth of Provera, an artificial hormone meant to cause the uterus to shed its lining of blood. The idea was to see if my body could still menstruate. I obediently took the pills. My uterus shed its lining of blood.

That was the extent of my physical treatment: speculum, swallowing hormones, lightly bleeding for two days.

The doctor opened my virgin body to peer inside but what the anorectic needs is someone to whom she can open her mind. Speculum of language to enter into unseen thought.

My mind was still a white kite in space, living on its dream to fly.

When the body is in a state of starvation, the mind becomes sharp and clean as ice. When hunger is denied, the ambivalence of feeling is eclipsed. There is no conflict, no uncertainty, because you are skating on the edge of that ice, round and round, tracing your own end.

My anorexia was a removal of form, and of former thought. It was an unflinching search in the night so as to become an author of night.

A denial of desire in the search for desire. Losing as a way of finding something out.

I lost my way on purpose—like Gretel, the one who left no trail of breadcrumbs behind. I went into that dark wood that lies at the edge of what we know.

In that wood I found the discovery of the wind and I claimed the silence of these words.

On that edge I witnessed pure emotion in a raw blue space. I saw a thousand birds taking flight and saw a thousand fish traveling in the sea. There was no delineation between earth and sky and my body existed outside of space and time.

This is the place where my hunger has led me. Everything is perfectly quiet. Now I have found writing to smooth the bones of hunger and quench the thirst.

The hunger for writing holds me in suspension between innocence and experience. I go into this page to get out of my body.

At seventeen, I could not imagine the flow of milk and blood that my body would become, the two little girls that it would nurture and produce. My body story at this age was a stealing in the night, a sheet of ice, a straight road in snow.

Duke University. The thick envelope informing me of my admission had arrived several months earlier. It fell through the mail slot with a thud, into the house on a bitter March day.

August 1984. My parents and my younger sister and I drive in the late summer heat through southern Ohio, West Virginia, Virginia, into North Carolina. Moving into a new place, moving into a new life. The air becomes moist and hot. In restaurants we choose: sweet tea or unsweet?

I bring a brown French-made bike on which I will speed from East campus to West and back again. No helmet, books slung over my shoulders, my heart yearning and free, 120 pounds.

I register for French literature, philosophy, oceanography, English. I make new friends. I attend class religiously, craving the textbooks, the notes, the ideas, the thought. I slave over Kant's *Critique of Pure Reason* in Perkins Library while my heart beats slowly and steadily in its light cage of bone. I drink in the French poetry I am assigned to read: it becomes a love affair. Rimbaud's drunken boat, Baudelaire's *Correspondances*—

> *La Nature est un temple où de vivants piliers*
> *Laissent parfois sortir de confuses paroles . . .*

How I loved the freedom, the silence and the lamplight in the East campus library, the supreme quiet of the brick walkways on the quad. Study and writing were sustaining my life.

I decide for certain that I will double major in English and French. Duke does not recognize the double major but I proceed anyway. I decide for certain to go to Paris during my junior year.

Twentieth-century American literature. This course opens me like a flower. I sit in the front row in a class with over a hundred students. The American dream and its failure written in verse on an empty piece of paper, the plain angles like the church pews in my hometown, or the clear panes of glass upon which no angels appeared.

Stevens's "The World as Meditation" still soothes me —Penelope waiting for Ulysses, who never arrives but is always approaching—*never forgetting him that kept coming constantly so near*—and in this *almost*, her desire flowers in the imagination, the only place where the reunion will ultimately occur.

My mind was awakening inside a body that was starving. My starving body had become my norm, the light canvas upon which my intellect was drawn, a transparent structure upon which to lay my thought. This part of the body story would continue for years with brief periods of reprieve and periods of relapse.

Most of the girls on my hall in my freshman dorm on East campus had some form of eating disorder or disordered eating. One of my new friends would come back to the dorm after class and eat an entire jar of peanut butter with her index finger, spooning it in while she told me about her academic stress and trouble with boys. Another new classmate, very tiny, hoarded food in her room in neat piles and ran miles and miles every day.

I remember boys and lots of fraternity parties. There was another close call with sexual assault, a kiss that turned into force, alone in a boy's dorm room, and again, my wrestling away from him. There was a walk in Duke gardens late into the night with a shy red-haired boy. Other invitations, other kisses that tasted of cheap beer. Pint-sized plastic cups with ridges near the top, the keg sputtering and releasing its foamy spoil.

During that year I received a minimal amount of counseling for the anorexia. I cannot remember how and why

I went for the sessions. Each student was entitled to about ten. I stopped after two. The woman to whom I spoke recommended that I read the book *Fat Is a Feminist Issue*. This book introduced me to the idea that my private experience of starvation was part of a larger cultural context. It taught me that something in the culture was conspiring, through this ideal of slenderness, to limit the possibility for women's authority, taking up space in the world.

The counselor referred me for a medical examination. The doctor who examined me became very focused and angry with me. He yelled at me for several minutes. He yelled that my body would soon begin to metabolize its own muscle, having no more fat to spare. His voice was forceful, authoritative, adamant. White doctor's coat and stethoscope. Comparing my weight to that of concentration camp victims, the doctor protested that I might not be able to bear a child.

I was nineteen. My mind was as clean and neat as the edge of a page, my thoughts as quick as computer keys racing along. I was startled by this doctor's anger. His scare tactic worked to an extent. I thought about my body burning its own muscle. I began to eat a bit more, coaxing my weight higher than 120 pounds.

During my sophomore year I fell in love again. The heart's light has so many secrets and curves. Then the heart's shadows enclose it in the dark. He fell—hard—in love with me too. Christopher. Born in Hong Kong on the top of Victoria's Peak, father a missionary, mother a writer and artist. This is my husband, the father of my daughters.

I do not know how to speak now of the breaking down and the healing, the southern heat and the Christmas trees, the communion and reunion, separation and loss, and the way that my story with him continues.

Paris

1987. January. Turning twenty-one, I travel alone to Paris. I want to go for the entire academic year, but my college sweetheart cannot bear to be separated that long. I agree to just one semester. I have waited so very long for this.

I need to cross this ocean in the night, to another life, to another form, to find another part of me. Some expression to show me a new way.

I am twenty-one years old. I began learning French when I was eight. French has almost always been deep within me. It has come to mean a seduction, a freedom, another way, another space.

In the weeks before boarding the transatlantic flight, my father gives me extra attention, walking up and hugging me with tears in his eyes. My parents did not travel abroad until middle age. They traveled to England and left us with my father's parents. When they returned, they brought us doll figures of guards at Kensington Palace. There was something new in their eyes. I noticed it at age ten and I wanted it.

Paris represents a space of peace in my body story. As a student there I am free, unencumbered, my mind takes flight and my body feels calm.

The baggage workers were on strike the day that I landed, and Paris was buried in snow. I had never felt more alive. The striking employees had merely heaped hundreds of suitcases in a giant mound, leaving each passenger to fend for herself.

I choose to live in an apartment rather than with a French family. I need autonomy and the key to my own door, my own space and the time in which to claim it.

I share an apartment with another Duke student, an American from Pittsburgh. We are different, we have fun, I study more than she does, she kisses more boys than I do.

I register for courses: Paris IV (Sorbonne), Paris VII (Jussieu), the Institut Charles V. Literary representations of Paris in French literature. Advanced composition. British literature, taught in English. I am called upon as the model to recite D. H. Lawrence since I am a native speaker. The French students look over their shoulders quizzically at me. I continue to recite Lawrence's virile, passionate words in my bland, American English.

At the Sorbonne I am relatively anonymous. I sit contentedly in the *amphithéâtre*, taking notes, observing, listening to the lectures on Aragon and Apollinaire. I chat with some French students but I never really blend in. It is not because of my language—I am at home in French.

No, it is something else, *autre*, a longing, a tug or pull, a solitude, a center of silence that no one can ever know. Michigan birch and stone. As a child my nickname was "pensive little one."

My time in Paris was a gold box, an opening, a revealing of possibility. My body suffered less as I followed my mind. I had all the time in the world; time moved in me and I sailed in it.

Art becomes the central meaning of my life. I spend hours upon hours in the Musée d'Orsay, refurbished train station, gorgeous iron hands of an immense clock through which I gaze at pristine cream statues, reclining nudes, Rodin's *Gates of Hell* and *Head of Camille*. I am in awe.

With my student card I gain free entry to the Louvre. I walk through it time and time again, miles in all, a quiet, steady pace. Sometimes I have entire salons to myself: attending the crowning of the empress Josephine, floating with the *putti* in violet clouds, contemplating a tombstone in Arcadia.

I walk on creaking parquet floors as my fingers absent-mindedly caress the red velvet ropes draped between heavy brass stands. I disappear into Watteau's delicate, wistful scenes: *Pélerinage à l'île de Cythère*. Are these figures arriving for their idyll or departing in regret? Their meaning is an enigma, their elusive suspension in time between what has been lived and what is yet to come.

I have flown above the blank Midwestern fields, each one a lovely bare page upon which to imprint pure thought. I watch the cold Seine endlessly, its steely swells and the secrets they hold, the massive stone *quais* separating the water from its urban home, the *bouquinistes*, a language that I am learning to call my own.

Paris offers me a respite from the starvation. My eating returns to a semblance of normality. I gain weight but I do not really notice. I get my period. I sleep deeply. My hair grows long.

Rue vieille du Temple, in the Marais. Discovered on my own. Ancient Jewish quarter. Hot falafel sandwich in a half-moon of pita, with pickled purple cabbage and tahini sauce. *A emporter.* I hand over my thick coin and am handed the food. I walk and peer and read this city, the history of the *quartier*, Orthodox Jewish boys in dark shorts and white shirts, paying no heed to me as they play.

I walk endlessly through the city, a *flâneur*, discovering impossibly serpentine streets and outdoor markets, the poultry in cages just as Baudelaire described them, the round marble tables, the indescribably delicious *café-crèmes*, golden sweet hot foam and rectangular sugar cubes.

I am independent, moving in my body, and free. Paris is pure seduction.

I get drunk on art. *Enivrez-vous: de vin, de vertu, ou de poésie.*
Sometimes I stand for at least half an hour in front of a
single canvas. Van Gogh's irises, Van Gogh's bedroom. I
stand in front of them so long that my thoughts become
part of their texture—the stretch of the canvas, the imme-
diacy of the stroke. Purple, deeper purple, deepest purple,
bluest sky. The line of each iris an evocation of sorrow. The
narrow bed, the open window, and the chair. The pathos
of the moment when the paint touches the canvas. The
dampness, the smell of oil and turpentine, the eye guiding
the hand to lay down the paint.

This is pure living, this is the force of living. I eat when
I am hungry—four o'clock, nine o'clock. Glasses of wine,
warm baguette. My long legs carry me wherever I want
to go.

I travel to Amsterdam, Lausanne, Bologna. I ride a bus
all night long to see Amsterdam. I visit the Anne Frank
Museum and I am reduced to pure reverence and a state
of grief. I nibble on a hash brownie and doze on the bus
all the way back to Paris.

In Lausanne with my roommate, I watch swans floating on the lake. We sleep on crisp cotton feather duvets and
subsist on fresh milk chocolate. In Bologna I walk through
incandescent sunlight filtering among the gorgeous ar-
cades. I do not have enough money to reach my desti-
nation, Florence. My roommate goes ahead and I must
return, alone. I ride a train through Italy standing up all
night, my slim body pressed against so many Italians returning north from their Easter in Rome. *Buona Pasqua,* I
learn to say to them. *Quanta costa? Grazie. Prego.*

This is my life: body and mind reconcile, commune.
Speed of the *métro.* My apartment near the Mosque, 1 bis
rue des Quatre fages. I hear the song of Muslim prayer

Starving Body

chanted in the morning and in the evening. Near the Jardin des Plantes, the rue Mouffetard, the rue des Ecoles.

My apartment in the fifth arrondissement is situated above a Renault Elf garage on a street too small to be depicted on some Paris maps. From its windows, I watch pigeons, clothes on a line hanging in the urban air. Above, the sky and the *rondini* twittering and twirling together, black and spare, dotted lines tracing mysterious text against the changing light.

Stolen kisses. American boys traveling abroad, smiling at me and my roommate across the restaurant in the heart of the Latin quarter. Catholic Midwestern boys from Notre Dame, Indiana. I show one of them how to climb over the ledge along the Seine, crouching on the massive stone just above the gray swells below, the ancient movement of the water. There he borrows a light embrace from me while the gargoyles of Notre Dame de Paris watch in stone.

Eric. A French boy I meet through other friends. He lives in Blois and I visit him and his parents. He gives me a tour of the château in Blois, the former residence of François 1ier. I watch him play tennis. We visit Chambord. After a long period of conversation and visits we share a few deep kisses. That is all. It is spring in France. The sun is delicious and the leaves a deep green.

Un crêpe banane-nutella ordered at midnight after going out with my roommate. The crêpe starts out as thin liquid on the pan's round surface, then bubbles up in thin, crisp sweetness as the cook spreads it around with a rubber blade that resembles a car's window wiper. The young man then spreads it with chocolate-hazelnut sauce and fresh banana, twists and twirls it, and wraps it in white paper.

Hot and sweet. I hand him my thick ten-franc coin—
merci bien. I am on my way, descending the rue Mouffetard,
peering into its shops with their postcards and books, the
Greek restaurateurs smiling at me with their hands raised
as they boast of their fares.

I read and reread e. e. cummings. I read in French
about Carson McCullers's *séjour* in France. To find some
comfort in my native English, I frequent Shakespeare and
Company, the English-language bookstore nestled in the
shadow of Notre Dame.

Deep within my anorexia I had been trying to leave
something behind. Now Paris enabled me to leave, to get
beyond that something, without losing myself along the
way.

Like my body's language and the language of my
thought, I was living a duet between English and French.
That duet, that seduction, continues to this day. Not being
able to have one without the other. The two languages like
two lovers, two hearts, inside and outside, center and edge.

My British literature professor was earnestly dedicated
to his work. Physically disabled, he walked painstakingly,
with a limp. He is another life that helped me to live mine,
another mind that reached out to me. I still recall the
authors he opened to me—Katherine Mansfield, D. H.
Lawrence, James Joyce. I still pick up my collection of
Mansfield's stories, *The Garden Party and Other Stories*. The edges
of the pages are turning yellow and crisp, my pen marks
inside going from blue to a different violet.

Joyce and *Ulysses*. Molly's monologue. I was not able,
am still not able, to master this difficult work. And yet this
dear man, the professor in Paris whose name I can no
longer recall, who was an expatriate living in Paris, like
Joyce, this lovely man with the stiff, uneven gait revealed

to me in teaching this work the possibility within language of getting beyond each day's lack of meaning, each moment's loss.

Somewhere, in the stacks of folders and notebooks that I have kept, I might find that teacher's name folded among the papers that I wrote, by hand, in English, during that spring in Paris in 1987, my respite from starvation, the nurture of my mind.

Molly. A woman of flesh and blood and milk. A woman of anger and frustration and desire. A woman created in the mind of a man and communicated in a language that surpasses the limitations of grammar and convention. This state of *dépassement* showed a freedom to me.

Molly's monologue inscribes her body, the imagination and mobility of female desire, captured and expressed by Joyce's literary genius, an example of language overthrowing its own constraints in the center of its power—

yes so we are flowers all a woman's body
I asked him with my eyes to ask again yes and then he asked me
would I yes to say yes my mountain flower and first I put my arms
around him yes and drew him down to me so he could feel my breasts
all perfume yes and his heart was going like mad and yes I said yes I
will Yes
and yes I said yes I will Yes.

(Joyce, *Ulysses* 643, 644)

June in Paris, 1987. My parents come to visit and to help me cross the English Channel with my bags. My father climbs to the top of Notre Dame cathedral with me. Vast violet stone, decades of soot, stone steps worn smooth by millions of feet. My mother stays below, a dot among the throng standing unevenly on the ancient, gray *parvis*. We wave to her.

Our visit is awkward. I want to feel closer to them but I do not know how.

The day we leave, I cry hard in the taxicab that takes us to the train. I do not want to leave Paris, I have not had my fill, I am still hungry for its seductions, for Degas's pastels of dancers in the Musée d'Orsay, kept in half shadow like the secret of thought. The body of my mind is still so hungry, craving one more view of Manet's *Déjeuner sur l'herbe*, the bold gaze of the female nude who challenges the spectator to contemplate her subjectivity as well as her body.

I have not had enough of the bridges—the Pont Neuf, the oldest bridge in Paris, the pure romance of the Pont Alexandre III, gilded dream—or the delicate tipped points of the Ile de la Cité and the Ile Saint-Louis, city bosom.

I leave this sustenance of stone and book, the trace of pastel, stained glass, hot coffee with cream, *petit pain au chocolat*.

I cross the Channel with my parents. They show me the white cliffs of Dover. They seem so stark and spare, like the drifts of snow of my becoming.

I settle into summer study at New College, Oxford University. My parents say goodbye. My college sweetheart is there on scholarship. I have convinced my parents to let me study there too. I will make progress on my English major.

I am reunited with my college sweetheart. His auburn hair shines against the light of his clean white shirt. Our bodies find each other again, his eyes speak of the meaning of green.

He and I travel through Cornwall, all the way to Land's End. Sweet scones with clotted cream. Sherry served in little transparent cups.

My plan of study is British literature. T. S. Eliot. Wilfred Owen. W. B. Yeats. No woman writer was ever assigned to me during my formal undergraduate study. No Jane Austen, no Virginia Woolf.

My room looks out over marvelous green lawn and gold stone. I have a sitting room with a piano, and a small bedroom. For my baths I must walk down the hall. There is no shower. My sweetheart sleeps with me in my small bed. During one of the two months, my period is late. I spend two nights dreaming of the unconscious, absent child, how he would look, how she would move. Then my period comes. I cry tears of relief.

The American students conform their study to the Oxford tutorial. In my section, modern literature, there is an odd number of students. This means that one student will meet alone with the tutor to discuss the weekly readings individually. I volunteer. The craving is strong. If I can have the personal instruction I want to make it mine.

My tutor's name is Julian. Julia and Julian. He is young, bespectacled and bearded, distracted by sculpted lines of verse: *Come from the holy fire, perne in a gyre.* I read and absorb every word he assigns. For the weekly tutorial I go to where he resides. While he presses me to interpret Eliot and Yeats, his young, pregnant wife periodically peeks in on us. He is engaged with me in the seduction of metaphor and idea. She checks on us with the straight line of her gaze. I keep my eyes on my open book.

Oxford returns me to English, to the beauty of my native language, its spare center, its lesser ornament. French is circular and embellished, decorative to look at and luscious to speak. English is linear, more utilitarian, and therein it finds its beauty—the plain land of my origin, my home.

In Paris I had absorbed French to the point of fluency, dreaming in it, thinking in it, inhabiting its beauty and mastering its precision. I had gotten to the point where my mouth felt strange forming words in English.

My tutor Julian, the piano in my room, my college sweetheart, and modern British literature. T. S. Eliot. I reread today, so many years later, my careful, penciled notes in the facsimile edition. *The Waste Land*. Its most beautiful line,

> *These fragments I have shored against my ruins*

Here is freedom, here is language freed from both body and mind. My tutor devoted his time and talent so that I might understand this. No punctuation, no inhibition, nothing superfluous, nothing unclaimed.

The facsimile reveals the cutting down to pure essence. Ezra Pound—il miglior fabbro—knew that pure expression must be created at the limit of presence.

Is this what my body knew, the reduction to pure form? Pound cut entire columns of Eliot's poem. I still crave this reduction of pounds.

Poetry and writing as the means of an opening. I sit here now, an early spring day. Spring is late this year in coming to Atlanta. The weather has been strange. The branches are still bare and dark. Easter is merely weeks away. The branches trace a text against the gray lid of sky.

Until my graduate study, I read—almost without exception—male writers because that is what I had been assigned. Chaucer. Shakespeare. Rimbaud and Baudelaire. Joyce. Lawrence. cummings. Aragon. Apollinaire. Owen. Eliot. Yeats. I went into their talent through self-determination.

I read the women on my own: McCullers, Plath, Sexton, Millay. *A Room of One's Own* by Virginia Woolf.

Plath killed herself. Sexton killed herself. Woolf killed herself.

How did the warmth feel? The towel rolled under the door? How did the fur coat feel as the engine started to purr? How did the cold water feel, waist, shoulders, and neck?

There is a possibility. Do we not all ponder this at times? Then consciousness cuts in with its bare bodkin of "why." The dreaming and the sleeping. I have taken Woolf's admonishment to heart. I have a bit of money and a room of my own.

You must not give in to the sleep of reason. You must take your body and fold it into your mind.

> *Who is the third who walks always beside you?*
> *When I count, there are only you and I together*
> *But when I look ahead up the white road*
> *There is always another one walking beside you*
> *Gliding wrapt in a brown mantle, hooded*
> *I do not know whether a man or a woman*
>
> (Eliot, "The Waste Land," lines 360–65)

Relapse

I still consider the emptiness, the high that true hunger brings. I like to run three miles when my body is light and feel the steady pounding of blood and bones. My hands still seek my hip bones, the secret composition they form with my ribs.

The moment of my writing corresponded to the time of my starvation. Poetry was the first form in which I wrote and it remains my abiding desire.

The poem takes language down to its essence, to a spare refinement, an inscription that neither demands nor receives. A fine poem exhibits no excess and leaves the reader with nothing beyond the certainty of its fleeting elegance: *Nothing that is not there and the nothing that is* (Stevens, "The Snow Man").

So too it is with the anorectic's willfully thin body. The body becomes a poem that displays its finest form, its strong but cool structure, its restraint, its encounter with silence as the limit and truth of physical expression. Both are like the dream eclipsing linear thought within the unconscious mind.

My body-of-absence is a dance of purest movement through space, unencumbered, undone, remarkable in its ability to arrive and then move silently away.

It is a kind of returning to a girlhood grace—the diver, the ballerina, going trick-or-treating, skipping, playing hopscotch, climbing my favorite tree.

Losing myself in the pursuit of this weightlessness, I can try to hide from separation and loss. The starving body longs to experience the physical form at the limit, as the limit. Like the poem in which nothing is left wanting and what is desired is its own end, hunger seeks out desire in the negation of desire and finds its fulfillment in the refusal of its need.

I take a break from this writing to respond to my body's hunger. This is something I am only beginning to learn. On this particular day, I have run three and a half miles and up until now I have eaten about eight M&Ms, one animal cracker, and a banana. Not a good day.

I go to the student center at the college where I work. Getting money at the ATM forms a part of this necessity, the obligation to eat that I can no longer escape. I choose French fries and a small scoop of tuna salad with pickles and onions. No roll—too much carbohydrate. I allow myself to consume half of the fries. I eat all of the pickles and onions—crunch and salt with virtually no calories. As I ingest the tuna salad, my thoughts fold into and within each other in a tangle of form. I reassure myself that I need protein but the tuna tastes sickening. Halfway through the last bite, I cannot keep going. I spit it out. I stand quickly and throw away the uneaten food. Styrofoam plate, napkin, and plastic fork crumple together with the uneaten food and disappear into the trash bin.

Sometimes I still slip from moderately healthy eating into restriction.

I relapsed while I was on full scholarship for summer study at the Institut d'Etudes Françaises d'Avignon. I was a graduate student. It was 1992. I was almost finished with my master's thesis on theatricality in Baudelaire's *Tableaux Parisiens*.

Before I had children, I traveled on my own in Switzerland and Paris on a dissertation fellowship. I was twenty-six and had been married three years. I was terrified of gaining weight while in Europe so I restricted my eating drastically. Looking back I see that this restriction was very dangerous; at the time I saw nothing wrong.

As I researched Rousseau at the University of Geneva and visited Voltaire's former residence Les Délices; as I climbed to the top of the cathedral in which Calvin preached and explored every bookstore in Geneva's old city, I slipped quickly back into anorexia nervosa.

The compulsion to restrict my food intake still catches me unaware.

Writing this story is allowing me to get past it.

During that trip I drank herbal laxative tea every night. I put two teabags into the hot water instead of one. I remember tomatoes eaten with friends and being afraid of all the food my friend's new French bride was offering to me. I remember tastes of Swiss chocolate. By the end of my two-week trip the accumulated effect of the laxative tea had overtaxed my system. I was suffering from severe diarrhea that I could not stop. I had absolutely no appetite because my body had turned off the switch of its own hunger in an effort to preserve itself. Weak and afraid, I was too ashamed to talk to my friends.

Somehow I have felt for a very long time that the eating disorder was my fault and my blame. The guilt was so entrenched that I failed to see it.

Alone, I walked into a Swiss pharmacy and asked for help. Outside the pharmacy was the green neon sign shaped like a plus sign and signaling me in.

Again, I was fortunate. The pharmacist gave me some medicine and talked with me. He explained how I must stop drinking the tea. He complimented me on my fluency in French, noting that he had heard very few Americans speak so well and with such ease.

When I returned home to America and to my husband, I stepped on the scale. My weight was about 125. I had lost six pounds in two weeks and was utterly exhausted.

My husband and I were living in New Mexico, where he was doing research and I was writing my dissertation. It took me a week to rest and rebuild my strength.

Still, I was unable to talk about it. I simply told my husband that it was jet lag. That I was exhausted from the trip.

That remote place of snow inside my mind was still lost to me. I could not tell my story, even to my husband.

There was another relapse when I began my tenure-track job as assistant professor of French in Atlanta. This one lasted for at least a year. Again, I denied my struggle even to myself. The pressures of teaching advanced content (literature of the French Enlightenment) in French for the first time, earning the main household salary, and being scrutinized as a new colleague at a small college proved too much for me to bear.

I retreated into restriction. My weight again fell below 130. My metabolism was a relentless furnace, burning everything I ate as rapid fuel. I could not locate the rhythm of my natural appetite because my body was absorbing and utilizing energy so fast.

Anorexia is a chronic affliction that keeps complex secrets. It has its own language that is known only to the initiates of the disease. When my body retreats into deprivation my mind absolutely resists what it does not want to see. I can come up with lots of ways to seem okay.

It has taken me nearly twenty years to write this.

Anorexia is a way of speaking about strength and about vulnerability. It is a way to put some distance between the (desired) body and the world. Being underweight is a way to protect yourself from overwhelming demands.

Starvation is a form of communication that offers the body as a text to be read. Its message articulates a subtle cultural protest.

The protest concerns the societal ideal. The anorectic effaces herself in pursuit of the physical ideal, but in so doing she succeeds too well at the game. Her emaciated form reveals the oppression of thinness by manifesting a dangerous exaggeration of this ideal.

The sexual assault that I suffered at the age of twenty occurred at a time when I was not terribly underweight.

I was energetic and I had gentle curves. That assault may have prompted my relapses into weight loss.

When you are healthy and therefore desired, you have to negotiate the intrusions of words, hands, honking horns, and the gaze. Starvation allows you to step out of the game and to know your mind and its desires.

Has the time of deprivation come to an end? I have lived inside a body of snow, a body of absence, a body of wind.

5 WEDDING BODY

It is May of 1988. A lovely North Carolina spring. The fragrance of tobacco is in the air. Downtown Durham is quiet and unchanged.

I graduate from Duke University in May and by the first of June I am engaged. My college sweetheart has returned from a trip to Saudi Arabia where his parents are living. He has a diamond ring in his pocket, a ring from a part of the world I have never seen. On bended knee he asks for my hand and places the ring on my finger.

We were both twenty-three. Fourteen years later, we are still married and are raising two young daughters.

We could not know of the children, the work, for richer or for poorer, the sickness and the health. We recited the vows but we did not understand that we would live them. We followed a green path pursuing love and a cultural script.

I could not have foreseen my relapses into starvation, the remote places where my depression would lead me, the breaking down that would become this journey of writing, this story that is returning me to the garden I once knew.

June 1988. College graduates. Newly engaged. We move to New York. I have my first paid job in publishing as a marketing assistant, Oxford University Press. He teaches high school in rural Connecticut. I take the train into Grand Central from Greenwich each day. We rent part of a pink house on a quiet street.

At my first job I communicate with offices in Tokyo, Durban, Oxford UK. It is terribly exciting even though I am nothing more than a glorified secretary. My pay is abysmal. My fiancé and I go out to dinner once in a year. When we spend time in Manhattan, we buy coffee in blue paper cups and walk in Central Park.

On the train, I read *Bride's* magazine. Although I want to resist the images, I am enthralled by the radiant brides, the simulacrum of their charm. When I was a teenager I would pore over sweet sixteen girls in size four pleated skirts and blouses. Now, engaged, I study these perfect brides in size six gowns. I even recognize some of the same models.

I have only a minimal role in planning my wedding. My mother and older sister still live in Cleveland and they make most of the arrangements. When my fiancé and I go there for Christmas we make a few choices. Everything seems fine. We decide to honeymoon in Québec.

We invite one hundred people and order engraved invitations. My parents request the honour of your presence. My mother says the u in *honour* was a mark of refinement.

During this time my mind and body were somehow

disconnected, resisting the institution of marriage in subtle ways. I did not want the honeymoon to be a surprise. He and I planned it together. I did not want to cover my face with a veil. I did not want to change my name. Some of my resistance was accepted; some of it was met with opposition.

In the end, I did change my name.

Although my body was a woman's, my mind was still imprinted with the echoes of an unfinished girl. Those echoes spoke of persistent loneliness, depression, deprivation, anorexia nervosa, sexual intrusion.

I tried not to hear them. Later they would insist.

Focusing on the event of the wedding allowed me not to listen to them. I became preoccupied with the invitations, the dress, the flowers, the maids' gowns.

The bridesmaids each wore a different color. Their dresses were custom made. Pink, blue, palest green. The wedding was set for June 24. I was to be married in the church in which I grew up. It is a congregational church. There are pews in straight rows and tall transparent windows. Nowhere is there any stained glass. I remember growing up, looking at snow and black branches through clear panes of glass. I remember the plain wood of the pews and the distant organ pipes in perfect rows.

Our wedding was to be in the chapel, which had a black-and-white-checked floor. This detail seemed almost glamorous to me in comparison with the sanctuary's vast empty space. The chapel was intimate and tucked away in the top of the church.

The cake was ordered, my fiancé's favorite kind. The reception was arranged in an old mansion in Cleveland that had become a social club. My family had never joined such a club. A few times, though, I had gone to dances with my high school boyfriend. I remember the teenage girls and boys, their easy affluence, their elegant clothing and clean white hands. At one dance I wore a wonderful dress of iridescent blue taffeta and deep midnight velvet. I felt just as pretty as the other girls.

December 1988. I went with my mother and sisters to shop for my gown. My mother had scouted out places advertising low prices. It was midwinter—Christmastime —and we drove for quite a while in the snow. The Midwestern sky was a blank expanse of gray, menacing in the nothingness that it revealed.

Trying on wedding dresses. They hang in rows on metal bars, gleaming silks and satins, clouds of tulle, scalloped hems and trains with hooks, sequins, pearl beading, crystal clasps.

If I could have I would have become one of those dresses—just as I wanted to become a white angel in the snow. I did not want to be the body in the dress. I wanted to be the dress—a pure form of lightness, without uncertainty, without weight and desire and instability and blood.

I wanted to be in that transparency, in the promise proclaimed by satin and tulle. I wanted the clean feeling found in those dresses on racks, the truth of their nonexistence, like the birch trees or the drifts of snow.

My body and my emotions felt heavy, opaque, unclear, unformed.

Is this not the symbolism of the wedding body—to place the opacity of the body, its mystery and mortality, into the dream of the white gown, its form of purity, its gathers and folds of lightness and light, its grace and delights, so that the marriage might begin with the promise of this lovely vision?

The bride stepping into the wedding gown is a woman stepping into that promise, trying to eclipse the ambivalence of the real with a gown of mystery and beauty.

My future husband was tall, dark, and handsome. He was brilliant and he was passionate, generous, and kind.

A veiled angel, the wedding body is a sign shrouded in the unwritten page of its most delicate fabric text. It signifies something that will never exist.

To avoid wearing a veil over my face, I chose a circle of artificial flowers with tulle and ribbons that cascaded down my back.

No one can touch the wedding body and no one can transgress it. No male may see it before the moment of its appearing. It is an apparition—clean, virginal, elegant, beyond language, communicating purely in a visual realm.

When the wedding body appears, everyone stands.

It is your moment, yet you cannot understand it all. You present yourself to those who have come. You join your life to another. That is the only part you understand. Within all of this you cannot locate yourself. Past and future fold in on the present moment. Everything is space and light and the feel of your gown.

The bride is spectacular in the true sense of the word. She is a pure object for the gaze. As such she is necessarily and unwittingly blind to herself.

Blinded in the lightness, in the white.

Blue eyes and dark blonde hair and manicured hands and dark pink lips.

Tall and graceful. Five feet ten inches. One hundred thirty-five pounds.

Fragrant and lovely, cradling in her arms the fresh, pale blooms where one day the children will lie. Later my body will flower and bloom with one child, then a second.

The moment is fleeting. Its transparency is captured compulsively by the camera's lens. The meaning of the wedding moment is "here-and-then-gone." The instantaneous moment is its own self-reflexive meaning.

The wedding body captures the instant of a dream: the perfume of flowers, the rustle of a virgin gown that will be taken off within hours and never worn again.

It exists solely in a space of memory and in the repetition of a dream. The bride lives in a moment of present memory, creating her own loss as the heart of her meaning.

She signifies the folding of an illusion within reality's hold.

You look at photos of your wedding body and you remember the loveliness that so soon was gone. Memory is imprinted by the transience of the wedding body: the fresh flowers that fade, the dress so carefully removed.

The wedding body produces a momentary spectacle, a spiritual inscription of the female form.

June 24, 1989. There is an overflowing of flowers. Hearts unfold like flowers before Thee. Stringed instruments play. J. S. Bach. Among other musical compositions, my fiancé and I have chosen the performance of Copland's "Fanfare for the Common Man." A lone trumpet plays. It is one of the only aspects of the wedding upon which we insisted.

I have chosen the palest peach-pink shoes, for which I spent one-fourth of my meager paycheck in New York.

Fourteen years later, I still have them wrapped in tissue in a box. They have curved heels and cut-out designs and they button over the top.

Today, my wedding gown lies professionally sealed in a tomb of plastic in a large box with scrolled writing on top. It is hermetically enclosed so that one of my daughters might wear it one day, as she lives the bride's enigmatic moment, nobility of loss.

The wedding body connotes a kind of divinity—the ethereal, the angelic—and as such it necessarily heralds a kind of disappearance. The bride is a vanishing point, always receding, always momentary, never preserving any status within the real. She is pure image consumed by pure gaze.

These elements—ornament, gown, pale pink shoes —serve as theatrical costume for a one-time role.

As a cultural personage, the bride brings peace to all who behold her. The promise that she signifies is declared entirely through her stillness and her nonverbal grace.

Captured in time compulsively through the photographer's eye, she declares a moment of living that will never be subsumed by the grip of disappearance. In this sense she conquers death. And in the same way her meaning regresses into pure absence—the photograph the record of her very finite appearance.

Does her stillness, her pose for the camera, illustrate the cultural expectation of female passivity? Or does it elicit the contemplation required in the presence of beauty?

We see in this instant the bride standing beside her groom, who is clad in black. The bride's gown gleams and folds and is perfectly arranged to cascade down the steps in a silken swirl.

White and black, bride and groom. Which color is life? Which color is death? The child—the union of life and the beginning of a death—arrives to combine both.

The bride is mostly silent and mostly still. These facts are not without meaning.

Her father walks her down the aisle and gives her to the groom.

&

The wedding body combines innocence with experience. The bride knows enough to pledge her love to another. Yet her body—her gown, her flowers, her stillness and grace —communicates an important and silent message of innocence.

My wedding body was a beginning. It was an encounter with beauty, an expression of pure form. It was a page upon which my adult life would be written. It was a mystery that would one day carry new life.

I could not have known what lay ahead. No bride ever could.

There was a toast to my beauty. Singing and dancing. Gifts with silver bows stacked in a pile. The champagne glasses were raised. I was vanishing within the collective gaze. I was seated next to my best friend, *amant*, the man to whom I had opened my body's deepest desires, the man who understood my desire to write, to write myself back to the garden of selfhood, of green shade and light, the man who would accompany me through childbirth, through depression, through the next part of this story.

Time Warp

Christopher and I move to New Mexico for two years in 1994. He has been offered a two-year, predoctoral fellowship. I am going to write my doctoral dissertation in the middle of the New Mexico desert.

I have finished my master's thesis on Baudelaire, have transferred advisors and fields of specialization, and am now writing on the epistolary novel in eighteenth-century France. I have passed my PhD written examinations, proving competency in literary interpretation from the Middle Ages through the present day. I have supported my dissertation proposal outlining a theory of epistolary lyric during the French Enlightenment.

We leave the South in a rented U-Haul with Georgia peaches printed on the sides. Each peach on the truck is half my height and three times my width. Round and full and pink and orange.

Because we are towing our car behind the U-Haul, we are, literally as well as symbolically, unable to back up. We must cross most of the country—North Carolina to New Mexico—without ever moving in reverse. This is as comical as it is upsetting. We are, indeed, moving one way toward a new place with no possibility of turning back. We are leaving behind a certain ease, brick pathways and damp flowers, buying new books at the beginning of each semester.

Our U-Haul has no air conditioning and we are making this move in early summer. We drive past the canopies of trees, the porches hidden in shade, and head west. The truck is filled with our furniture, books, clothing, dishes. The sterling and crystal and china we received for our wedding. Wedgwood wild strawberry. We liked it because the pattern meandered across the surface of the china, the English garden as opposed to the French garden.

North Carolina, lovely place of my becoming, of writing, of losing and finding my way. Wisteria in spring, feather leaves tracing the trees. Falling in love and falling out of love.

By that evening we are crushed under an awful thunderstorm as we approach our friends' home in Birmingham, Alabama. The U-Haul with our car attached behind rocks and sways in the wind, and lightning strikes from all directions. We make it to our friends' home. They tease me about being scared by the storm. We have wine and I fall into the guest bed.

The next day we continue. Out of the South and into the West. Into this new expanse, this vastness, this huge page of desert on which I will write a birth. In Arkansas the vegetation starts to fade. Then we spend a day and a half driving through the Texas panhandle. We stay overnight and park the car-truck contraption pointing west, since we cannot back up. We drink cold beer and eat Mexican food. The TV in the hotel room glares and speaks and flickers.

In Texas the sky turns into an inverted bowl. Our orange truck imprinted with the huge Georgia peaches is nothing against the land and under the sky. Something inside me catches with fear. I have agreed to this move but I do not know what to expect. We will be living seventy miles south of Albuquerque, in Socorro, the Spanish word for "help." I will write my dissertation in the desert in a town so small there is no café, no Kinko's, no clothing store, no mall. I have seen it before. The land and light are exquisite. The light travels over mesas, penetrates clouds, seducing the gaze and emptying human thought.

I don't know how I will write a dissertation on French

Wedding Body

women writers and epistolary lyric while residing in a tiny New Mexican town.

We arrive in Socorro. None of the china has broken. We will use it only once in the two years we live there. New Mexico is a new language, much more foreign to me than the French in Paris. The language here is a vocabulary of essence, of light, of pure color, the scent of juniper and the sharp smell of lightning.

Heat and violet-red waves of light. Orange mesa. Roadrunners scurrying across the highway. Cottonwood trees poised in an ancient stance. Arid sky. Yucca plants thrusting their once-a-year bloom. Dark hair, dark eyes. Brown and deep brown. Hispanic, native American. Cowboy boots and hats. Belt buckles bigger than my hand. Hammered silver with turquoise. Red or green chile? A new choice at the restaurant. Red chile is hotter and has a grainy texture, pure powdered heat.

Chile rellenos. Green chiles stuffed with cheese, dipped in batter, and deep fried. Negra Modelo beer. This is the best; it is dark and sharp and a tiny bit sweet. Sopaipillas—pockets of deep-fried dough served with honey at the end of the meal. Huevos rancheros, the dish my husband still likes. Sombreros and garish plastic flowers hanging on the restaurant walls.

This is a new seduction. A new language. I am afraid. I have no context for the land, the gaze of the sky, its vast blue stare. I want to give in to it but I do not know how. To embrace this I have to give up what I know.

Au revoir Paris, goodbye to the South. Goodbye to the museums with their faint smell of painted oils, canvases cradled in ornate gold frames, and statuary treasures of Greece and Rome. Stone hips and breasts, perfection of form. Goodbye to the verdant quad at Oxford's New College, the cloister in which I tucked my legs under me to read. Goodbye to North Carolina with its notebooks and pens, quiet library desks, commencement with its multitudes of blue gowns.

New Mexico is the earth split open to me, the sky dizzying in its ability to go on and on, without the boundary of trees, always leaping toward the horizon that seems to delineate the end of a life and the beginning of a life.

Boundless. Uncontained. How might I feel that free?

My body is going to split open here, to push out my first beautiful girl. The freedom is going to be hard to find. It is going to take a long time.

I am twenty-six when we move out West. I go running with my husband's colleague. He and I meet early in the morning before the heat sets in. We run free across the tops of mesas while he tells me about his girlfriend, far away. I notice him looking often at my legs.

I swim laps in the pool on the campus of New Mexico Tech. This is a small science-oriented university, a former mining school, and I have been hired as a lecturer in French. The pool, like the town, sits at the base of M Mountain.

At the end of each lap, I throw my legs over my head, dipping my shoulders and arms down deep into the water. I push off from the end with my hands pointed above my head. As I toss my legs above me, I see the solid turquoise sky like an opacity that also reveals, a space that also contains.

As I swim, my breath grows easy and deep. The sun is darkening my skin with every stroke and I will have deep tan lines after just twenty minutes. I am at an altitude of approximately ten thousand feet.

During this time in New Mexico I am not starving. My body is feminine and strong. I am going to become pregnant soon. 1995.

&

2002. Just now, during the writing of these pages, I pause to take a shower. I think of weighing myself but thoughts of this writing cause me to forget. This is such progress. Standing in the hot stream of water, my hands begin to glide over my body, a half-moon of blue soap cupped in my hand. No washcloth.

The soap travels my arms, my elbows with their corners of knobby bone, the secret places high inside my inner thighs, the trim form of my back. I try to accept the softer places, the stomach that has expanded twice for the growth and birth of my two little girls, the breasts that I have erased in the past, now fuller, having nursed those two little girls.

I step out of the shower and catch glimpses in the mirror as I dry off my dripping form. I want to encounter that solid turquoise sky, the horizon in my thoughts that lies so far away. Here in Atlanta, it is dark and rainy outside, though it is already midmorning. The sky is discreetly dull and utterly forgettable. Tree limbs have fallen during the night and my husband has had to clear them out of the driveway. I cannot see even a hint of horizon through the maze of trees and buildings and cars.

I see the plastic toddler toys in the wet yard next door. The mailboxes with crooked posts and metal flags. Trash cans stand in rows on the curbs. The next-door neighbor —father to five boys—opens the back window, throwing empty milk jugs forcefully into a green recycling bin.

The futility of these domestic sights is unsettling.

My thoughts return to the immense New Mexico sky, the bright water splashing as I push off for the next lap. I think of some trace of rhyme in ink or paint, something that might have grace and last

> *against the dying of the light.*

This tension—between futility and grace, between that which means nothing and that which might last—has played itself out in and through my body. The canvas of forming a child. The reduction to pure essence or the edge of disappearance and the flowering into life, the flow of warm milk.

I sit back down to this writing again. This writing is bringing me back to my body. These words are helping me accept my form, the round, soft places and the long, strong places, the clutch of memory and the present need.

෴

At New Mexico Tech, I am, not surprisingly, the entire French department. The unique opportunity for French in a predominantly Hispanic context makes me exotic. I teach one wonderful man who fought in World War II. He has passed away now. I can still see his handwriting, the wobbling scrawl he turned in to me without fail, conjugating the verbs, listening to his lab tapes, *je fais, tu fais, il/elle/on fait, nous faisons, vous faites, ils font, elles font.*

Along with the teaching, I write my dissertation. I email my doctoral advisor in Chapel Hill. I make pots of coffee and sit in our second bedroom—the room that will soon become a simple nursery with table and crib. Outside the scent of juniper and the electric smell, jagged bolts of light. I take our gray Saturn and drive alone to UNM-Albuquerque. I check out books for my research and stand for hours photocopying scholarly articles and sources.

Back in our apartment in Socorro, I synthesize what I have read. I theorize that the epistolary prose of this period reveals lyric elements more fully than the verse.

I sit and type as I am doing now. I crouch down on the floor and sift through stacks of articles and books. I mark and write in my primary texts. I color-code and highlight and back up on diskette. I love the work, the clean edges of paper, the bindings of the books, the art of their words.

I am extremely fortunate to have my new advisor. She allows me as much creativity as I need. She is the first teacher whose instruction truly makes me feel free.

My husband goes to his work every day, the Array Operations Center of the Very Large Array. He formulates the groundwork for his doctoral dissertation on star formation in H-2 regions. I of course do not understand much of this.

The comet strikes Jupiter. The astronomical community where we live is enthralled. There are special viewings with powerful telescopes. Jupiter hit and pockmarked, but still traveling its orbit in its ghostly, inhuman path.

6 GIVING BIRTH

November 1994. I have written about 150 pages of my dissertation. My husband makes a plea for a child. I hesitate, reluctant. I am twenty-eight. I know deep down that the transformation to motherhood is going to be a new path for my body, for my mind.

I agree to try, giving in to some instinct stronger than the boundary of my individuality. Pull of biological gravity.

By December 1 I find out I am pregnant. We have conceived Claire within three weeks of my agreement to "try."

Under that vast sky, in its cover of night, while Jupiter turned and the juniper lay still, our first daughter began to grasp life deep within the darkness of my form.

We travel to Chaco Canyon in the days right after Thanksgiving. Two cells have become twenty or thirty cells but I have not yet noticed a thing. We go there to get a few days away from work.

The Anasazi civilization reached its peak here between AD 900 and 1200. Of the Anasazi's multistoried homes, all that remains are the ghost circles of ruin, echoes of the marks left by the comet striking Jupiter. Pueblo Bonito, the most expansive, fully excavated ruin. Windows placed strategically for astronomical observation. The sacred *kivas*. Each a dark circle with an opening that reaches toward light. A form not unlike the womb.

With the bundle of human cells clinging inside me —my first child—my husband and I explore. We hike and climb, we dart in and out of the ruined homes. The Anasazi abandoned Chaco Canyon sometime around 1400. It is not known why. We walk high above the ancient organized town with its faint circles and paths. We stop to eat and drink on top of the grand mesas.

Petroglyphs. Animals with horns and delicate hooves. Spirals and constellations of lines. Messages now indecipherable to all but those who devote their lives to their study. Writing; leaving a trace.

> *Do not go gentle into that good night.*
> *Rage, rage against the dying of the light.*

Dylan Thomas wrote this poem and now we remember him through the reading of this trace. The Anasazi petroglyphs were scratched in artful earnest around the time of the first millennium; they too remind us that their creators were here.

Writing—the poet's anguished, drunken words, the Anasazi's quizzical spatial forms—is a rage against the dying of the light. An effort to resist the futility, the finite quality, the death. So is motherhood. The body can create its own way of writing.

I am trying now to record all of this, to leave some spare trace.

Giving Birth

The new text of my body has thus begun. In early December I take the pregnancy test with the first morning urine. There is no mistaking the blue line in the white square.

I confirm with the town's midwife. She puts the speculum inside me to examine me. I now think that was unnecessary. She tells me that an unmedicated childbirth is going to be good for me as a woman. I raise an eyebrow at her.

At the town library in Socorro I check out books on pregnancy. Riding home on my bicycle with the books balanced on my back and the tiny spiral of girl clinging inside, I suddenly become aware that a life is within me. I do not careen off the curbs as I would have done mere weeks before. Instead, I glide carefully and smoothly.

We tell our families at Christmas. They are thrilled. My mother tells me she will be happy for me in three months. She is trying to protect her own feeling of vulnerability; the first trimester involves the greatest risk for miscarriage.

Within a few more weeks the nausea sets in. It is a wave crushing me under, pressing me into my bed like shells pressed into the sand. I try the saltines, the soda water. I throw up in the late afternoon. Even television commercials for food provoke the sick, green feeling. I lose a few pounds. Until the fourth month of pregnancy I still wear my size six skirts.

There is overwhelming fatigue. Inside, my body is forming my daughter's heart, her eyes, her toenails, her spine. My books on pregnancy detail the growth day to day.

Food tastes awful. Coffee is sickening, everything is sickening. I eat plain rice and pasta and I choke down prenatal vitamins. Anemia is creeping in because the baby inside is taking all the iron from my blood. The anemia remains undiagnosed until after the delivery. Immediately postpartum, I will look as gray as the moon's powder surface.

After a few more conversations with the town's midwife I transfer my prenatal care to Albuquerque. I do not agree that a female must claim her womanhood through the ordeal of an unmedicated birth. I find an M.D. through my husband's health care plan.

My husband and I travel to Arizona so that he may attend an academic meeting. I am nauseated and exhausted most of the time. On our last day we visit Sedona National Park and we eat tuna sandwiches before driving back to Socorro.

Exactly eight hours after eating that sandwich I begin vomiting and cannot stop. In the middle of the night I awaken my husband and tell him I need immediate help. I am so weak that I cannot walk out to the car.

I am hospitalized with severe food poisoning. In my womb, my tiny child twirls and flutters. The nurse who administers IV fluids has trouble "getting a vein." Her attempts leave deep green bruises on the white inside of my left arm. I lie in bed for a day receiving intravenous fluids. The midwife comes by and reassures me about the pregnancy. At this point, she says, the fetus does not need much food at all, and gets everything it needs from me.

I go home and rest. I am so weak and my arm is so bruised from the botched IV that I cannot lift myself out of the tub. My husband lifts me out and helps get me into bed.

A few more weeks and I begin to feel strong. The fetus is developed; the spine is perfect, the heartbeat is strong. At around sixteen weeks we find out it is a girl. I am thrilled. I sit in the New Mexico warmth of a March sun and meditate with my hands on my hips. A girl. A girl. A wonderful girl.

I begin to gain weight. My energy comes back. My body is doing this. I feel her flutter and kick. I teach my French course and I write the conclusion for my dissertation. I set a date for the oral defense and plan to travel to Chapel Hill. My stomach ripens, beginning to show signs of the fruit it holds.

I crave lemons and potato chips. I no longer feel the nausea. I feel pretty and strong. Inside, the baby dances all day and into the night. In the deepest part of the night, she sleeps curled and quiet in her fluid while I sleep in my bed.

I mail the final copies of my dissertation to the committee in Chapel Hill. I have to go to Albuquerque to make the copies since there is no facility in town. I race across the mesas underneath the turtle sky. I am beginning to wear maternity clothes and my belly is growing a bit bigger each week.

Linea negra: the dark line that appears down the center of the pregnant belly. Like a secret trace or mark heralding the child within. That line has now come and gone twice on my body. It is a form of the body writing itself. It is like a stroke from some unseen calligraphic pen, thick and dark, something ancient, a question mark, an assertion, indicating the enigma of maternal form.

The blue veins that trace the surface of my pregnant breasts trace other questions, other bodily words. Meandering and intricate, a text of flesh that speaks of life and milk, an accompaniment to the rhyme of that dark line, violet blue *poème sans paroles*.

&

March 1995. I defend my dissertation in Chapel Hill wearing a black maternity suit with a velvet bow in the back. Before the oral defense, I sit for a while in Wilson Library on the campus of UNC. Long gleaming tables and wooden chairs, cases holding books like oysters cradling pearls. As I answer detailed theoretical questions about my dissertation, the baby turns her delicate pinwheels inside. After the defense, one of my male professors comments on the pregnancy, saying he'd thought I was expecting but wasn't sure.

August. During the last weeks of my pregnancy, I become nothing beyond my own pregnant body. I inhabit a new language for this body story, learning and using a new vocabulary of birth: *Is the baby engaged in my pelvis? Is she in vertex position? At what station does she lie? Am I dilating? Am I effaced?*

New words for a new story. Engaged means that the head is deep down in the pelvis. Vertex means that the baby is upside down. Your body has to dilate and efface before you can give birth.

Effacement, thinning out. Dilation, opening up.

Efface and open.

Push.

The New Mexico heat is searing. Our adobe apartment looks out onto open dirt and toward the small campus where I teach. During the windy months, the dirt lifts and blows in angry whirls. We have matchstick blinds to lower against the onslaught of the afternoon sun. Our swamp pump works hard to cool the rooms, circulating cool water, which then evaporates in the desert air. At this time of year in New Mexico it is a losing battle. On the plaza, the unemployed, the dispossessed, sit immobile in patches of shade, their faces obscured by their cowboy hats, their belt buckles shining in the glare of sun.

Since the eighth month of the pregnancy, I feel Braxton-Hicks contractions. The uterus practices for its magnum opus by bunching up and tightening itself in various places. Practice contractions. Sometimes they occur at regular intervals, seven minutes apart, six minutes apart.

A few days before the birth I am at once restless and exhausted, unable to go to the pool to swim laps. The spare bedroom in which I wrote my dissertation is now a simple nursery. Tiny diapers are stacked on a shelf and tiny clothes lie folded symmetrically in their clean drawers. Q-tips arranged in a cup, talcum powder ready for the first sprinkle on baby's skin. My thoughts about the birth are the exact opposite of this semblance of order: circling in wonder, scattered in fear, broken apart in sleepless nights.

August 18, 1995. Presbyterian Hospital, Albuquerque, New Mexico. I was admitted the day before for labor to be induced. I am past my due date. I spent the afternoon of the previous day seated in a birthing chair with Pitocin dripping into my vein intravenously. Still my body has not "progressed" from early labor to active labor.

My husband and I are alone together. No one from our family has come for the birth. Outside, the Sandia mountains bleed in the light, bathing in orange, yellow flame of August heat. The on-call obstetrician had criticized my admission on the evening before: "I don't know why your doctor admitted you to be induced. In my opinion you should just go home and wait." I have been pregnant for forty-one weeks.

The new meaning of my life is kicking and sleeping in my womb. My body is effacing and opening to let her out, but it just hasn't progressed into steady labor. In my faded hospital gown with the symmetrical cotton ties, white with a small pattern of blue, I begin to cry. The on-call nurse (there have been many) tells me to stop crying and be brave. I am given a sleeping pill and taken off the Pitocin. I ask about the effect of the pill on my daughter inside. My worry is dismissed by this frowning nurse. The pill sends me to a place of nonbeing, blank unconsciousness. My husband sleeps folded in a chair next to my bed.

August 18, 6 a.m. The sky outside is deepest pink, the color of my mystery. The baby and I have slept deeply because of the pill. Nurses came to check my blood pressure and the fetal heart monitor but I never woke up.

My regular obstetrician comes in to see me. "Where's the baby?" she asks cheerfully, teasing me with a shine in her eye. "Why didn't Dr. ___ just break your bag of waters? That is all that needs to be done and you will be on your way." I look at her, bleary-eyed and exhausted from the pregnancy and the sleeping pill, the anemia that has not yet been diagnosed.

My husband and I spend several hours agonizing over this difference of medical opinion: go home, or accept the advice of my obstetrician, who has followed the pregnancy with me. Once the waters are "broken," you are committed to the birth because of the chance of infection.

Late in the morning we decide to trust my obstetrician. The half-eaten hospital breakfast lies cold in its tray. The baby dances gently in my womb. My doctor comes in and places a long plastic hook inside me; it looks almost exactly like a crochet hook. I will recognize this implement three years from now, in Atlanta, when I am giving birth again, in August 1998.

She pokes and twists for a few seconds. I feel nothing. "Done," she says and tells me she will check on me soon.

Water. Womb water. Amniotic fluid. Tears of a woman's body. Ocean wave. Salt water starts to trickle out of me as I enter this suffering birth in the New Mexico desert. The trickle in between my legs increases to a gush. I am back on the Pitocin. It is time for this baby to come. The IV needle is cold and sharp in the vein on top of my hand. It is noon.

My husband is with me. Within an hour the contractions have reached a regular rhythm and my mind is transported to a place of pure physical endurance. In that place there is no language, just the deep pink of a nonexistent sky. Because this is my first baby, and because of my strength, I endure a lot of pain because I have no idea of how far I'm opening up. Ten centimeters is the magic number that allows a woman to push.

The contractions form their own language, communicating to my mind in a state of blank pain. I am buried by pain, I am swallowed by pain, I am submerged by pain, I am transformed by pain.

Giving birth feels like an encounter with destruction. Blood spatters and drips on the sterile tile floor. I think momentarily about the person who is going to have to clean it up. I stand, I bend, I sit. Then I cannot stand any more. I want the doctor to check me. I tell the nurse. The contractions crash my body into the bed. "I need to be checked, I need to be checked." I need a doctor to put his or her hand inside me to feel the opening of my cervix with a gloved hand. Is the opening two fingers wide? three fingers wide? I cannot stand this. When can I push?

I am told that the doctor will come to check on me "soon." The Pitocin courses through my veins, dripping into me through the vein in my hand. "Soon" means nothing to me right now. Time signifies only the duration of each contraction and the amount of relief in between contractions. Both seem like months or years, though they last only minutes. I am sailing through that sky of nonbeing.

Clinging to some edge of language, I continue to ask the nurse for the doctor's attention. I think her name was Marie, but I do not remember. It is 2 p.m. in Albuquerque, a Friday afternoon. Across the city, people are starting to think about leaving work. They are starting to think about a margarita, with salt, or their children, or the errands that need to be done. I am engaged in a lifetime of work that will inaugurate another lifetime of work.

Each contraction is a memory, a journey, a dream. Each one takes me to the center of my being and casts me away again. Into the space of nonbeing, back into the space of breathing, the place of this writing.

After an eternity, the doctor comes. As I write this now, almost seven years later, I cannot recall the doctor's name. My regular doctor has left her shift. The new doctor is a petite Asian woman with an intense, intelligent stare. She comes to check on me. We wait until the time between contractions. She tells me I am dilated to eight centimeters. I hear the nurse say, "I knew it." This nurse is essentially going to deliver the baby in about an hour. I beg for an epidural but the doctor says it is "too late."

"Too late" has even less meaning for me than "soon." The doctor and the nurse are speaking a language I cannot understand. My only communication is that of water, of blood, of pain. Tremendous pressure and enormous strength.

I am given an injection of Demerol to help "calm" me a bit and "take the edge off the pain." Even as I labor intensely and gaze at the doctor's steady face, I ponder the phrase "take the edge off the pain." I wonder if she has ever given birth.

There are words and then there is what the body says. All there is to the pain is the edge. This pain is pure edge, everywhere and nowhere. My mind is blank and at the same time it has never been more alive.

The doctor predicts that it will take two hours for me to dilate from eight centimeters to ten. My body, the shot of Demerol, and my mind. This moan of pain. After twenty minutes, I feel the baby moving lower into me. I tell the nurse I think it is time to push. She calls for the doctor, who is performing a cesarean in another room. The nurse checks me and confirms that it is time to push. She tells me that she always believes what the laboring woman says.

I talk to the nurse through the tremendous pressure and pain. The pregnancy guidebooks refer to this stage of labor as the ring of fire—the moment when the baby's head begins to push into the birth canal. These particular contractions produce a shock wave of suffering. I exist only in its force.

The nurse helps me into position to push. The Demerol has added a blur to my experience of the pain, like a piece of wax paper placed over my eyes. My entire body story at this moment centers on giving life to this tiny girl. I want to see her so badly—touch those fingers and toes, her wet plastered hair.

The nurse begins to coach me on pushing. The obstetrician will come when she finishes the C-section. PUSH! "One. Two. Three. Four. Five. Six. Seven. Eight. Nine. Ten. Good job!" I repeat this several times. My eyes are tight shut, focusing inward. I breathe, I gasp, I push, I am doing this, the baby is moving lower and lower, each contraction is an ocean wave of pain.

The doctor comes in

The baby is crowning now

Little wet dark-haired queen

Leaving behind the royal calm

Of the womb

With nothing more than her tiny form

Physical expression for the enigma of the soul

My body disappears and tears in the process of this birth. It is pure energy, pure strength, that mesa, that sky.

She is born.

An immediate, lusty cry.

We are naming her Claire Marguerite.

Seven pounds fourteen ounces. Twenty-one inches.

That final push—like the final push that I will exert three years hence, in Atlanta, giving birth to her sister— that final push is the untold rhyme, the book held in the hand, a circle of snow, the ornament hung on the pine.

She is wet and plump and wrinkled and divine. I cannot hold her because of the narcotic that went into my vein so near to her birth. I see her being lifted away from me, limbs flailing, tiny arms and legs forming two letter V's. I reach for her tiny wet hip as they lift her away, explaining that they must take precautions because of the Demerol.

Afterbirth. Do I want to see it? No, I respond. But out of the corner of my left eye I spy the doctor examining it for the clues it reveals, the nutrition it provided to the child in the womb. The only human organ that exists in order to be thrown away—red purple oval like some ghost of a forgotten story.

My stomach goes flat. My husband and the nurses comment on this. One nurse says, "She is going to be one where you would never have known she was pregnant."

I shake. My body begins to tremble and shake. This is common after childbirth. Nurses—unnamed angels—glide toward me with thick blankets to warm and calm. My legs jump and dance on the table with a life of their own.

A brief moment of respite—my torn and bleeding body buried in warm institutional blankets—did my mother go through this? All she said was, "You forget the pain." The forgetting is only partially true. Experiencing such pain changes you. The sky afterward is never quite the same, nor are the faces that you see in the streets, in cars.

My husband takes pictures of newborn Claire. She is lying under a heat lamp in her isolette, being rubbed and assessed by the nurses and neonatal pediatrician. My husband caresses her, talks to her—the gestures I want to do. She is getting her first shampoo with a hard plastic brush. I cannot take my eyes off her, a secret I've always known now being revealed to me.

She is so near, about eight feet away. Limbs tucked against her body as they were in my womb, curling and moving, forming closed and secret and lowercase letters, telling me a new story about what my life could become, a new body story for me to nurture and love.

Her newborn body offered me the enigma of its language, its beauty, its perfect newness. Her form allowed me to grasp her innocence, the lack of consciousness, the origin of a life.

Dark swirl of wet hair. Folded pink bottom. Newborn lungs breathing in, newborn eyes opening to the light. The fontanel, warm, soft, to which I place my index finger and feel the rhythm of her blood, see the pulse through the unclosed plates of her skull. This is the vulnerability of living.

My body is torn from pushing her out. The doctor tells me that the tear went three layers. She is sewing me up. Cold silver, local anesthetic. *Stitch. Stitch. Stitch. Stitch.* Dark thread moves through the air as the doctor works. Another text etched onto my body story, another suffering, another healing. The doctor explains that my daughter came out with her left fist held high, near her face—her salute to her own birth.

Nursing

Colostrum. Goldenrod, thick, this new fluid, rich gold, priceless, delivering immunities, antibodies from my body to hers.

Suck-suck-pause. Suck-suck-pause. Suck-suck-pause. Suck-suck-pause.

My newborn and I are alone. The adoring daddy is back at work. My mother has come briefly and gone.

You weigh eight pounds. You have your father's chin. Your round head with shell ears and the softly pulsing song of your fontanel, your unbelievable lashes, the bud of your lips, spring bloom, you are the most beautiful thing I have ever seen.

I am torn and bleeding. My breasts are aching and heavy with milk. Your little arms and legs curl against your body as they did in my womb. Newborn girl, you are my new story. I tuck you up to my breast, your little bottom cupped in my hand, and the milk "lets down," and it is warm, and white, and yellow, and blue, and it changes its configuration every time you nurse, sometimes more water, sometimes more fat, and I can tell the differ-ence, and you are drinking me in, telling me about who I shall become.

Heavy breasts. Warm milk. Newborn baby. Reflex to live.

You drink my mild substance until you are in a stupor. Your slate blue eyes close on the mystery of my becoming. You have discovered everything that hides inside me. You take a long nap on my chest, between my breasts, in the New Mexico heat. Outside, the violet mountain and a red sky flare and commune.

There is nothing that needs to be said. There is nothing between us that we need yet to understand. I have known you for a very long time and I am just beginning to know you. Your open mouth communicates a silent, blind faith.

I am frightened. You are frightened. I am in love. You are in love. You nurse again. My nipple is cracked and sore. I am new at this. Part of me begins to disappear, to fade before the conviction of your living.

You are patient with me. I figure it out—how to hold you, how to stroke your cheek with my light finger to get your head to turn at the right angle and then, just as your mouth opens, the milk is offered to you.

This is so elemental. A mother's body, sustaining the life of her child in flesh and warm milk. The Midwestern snow, the North Carolina spring, Paris with its gilded frames—these things are so far away. Now the map of my experience is measured by your ten toes, your pink fingernails no larger than printed words on a page.

What made you, what allowed you to roam in and through me, now drinking me inside? Nursing maintains our duet of intimacy. This intimacy demands that I exist merely for you. Now there are no books, no grades, no preoccupations, no arguments to be made. I exist for you to drink this milk and you exist to drink this milk.

Curious girl, angry at your own helplessness, curled as in my womb, you cry and fuss at the end of the day while the New Mexico sky dies in its vast color, oh violet, oh blue, baby's cries, you ride in your car seat, we all roll across these mesas while more milk stores up inside my breasts.

You are one week old, you are two weeks old, you are three weeks old, you are four weeks old. With each week I get stronger. You continue to take long naps on my chest, our siestas, our symbiosis, your milk, my milk, your taking, my giving, this eclipse of my form, this sacrifice of your becoming.

In the middle of the night, you come visit me in your daddy's arms like a royal guest, lying against my side, more milk, more milk, yellow gold in the middle of the desert night. Dawn. White-blue milk. Midday. Pure white. End of day, I am tired.

You are going to walk and sing and read. Your eyelashes are always going to captivate me. Right now you are eight pounds, nine pounds, ten pounds, eleven pounds. You take your bath in the kitchen sink. Your clothes are no longer than my forearm. You are a desert flower thrusting one bloom toward the sky. Your soul is a mesa, a circle of stones, a kiva in the dark with a hole of light.

The neat stacks of your clothes are like clean wings of doves. After I nurse you my shirt is covered with milk. My nipples heal. You and I have figured it out, this mutual language, this dance, your pressure, my yield, your question, my answer coming in liquid form.

You sleep a bit longer at night. Summer is turning into desert fall. My soul has deserted its former home. I am terrified, I am starving for you, I am so in love, I want to lay down my life for you.

Fall is coming. The desert is showing off its new light and you have new eyes with which to see it. The land shows off for you—blue, violet, deepest blue. Your eyes are the combination of all its colors.

I know you better than I know myself. It is always going to be this way. I can comfort you when I cannot comfort myself. You are my longing, the words that I can never quite say. Somewhere deep inside you seem to know this.

Shall I forsake you? Shall I turn away from you? Surely goodness and mercy shall follow me all the days of my life, little lamb, flash of light, you who moved so ceaselessly in my womb, you who seek the comfort of immobility at my breast.

I can take away all limitation in the name of your possibility. I have nothing to give you but the limit of my mortality, the lively stream of this milk that flows. In the suffering of our division we shall find our communion.

Look now at how strong you have become. See how my milk has given you the language of your smile. See how your daddy proudly holds you.

You are my breaking down and you are my building up. Beyond us both, the desert is stretching a canvas in dimensions far too vast to measure. Above us both, the sky is telling a story so ancient, so new, no one shall ever know. These are expanses against which our family means nothing. Our family means everything within this center of warm milk, your pajamas with feet, the winter coming on, your diaper and your crib.

I have been so afraid and I am still so afraid. My body has almost died and my body has created you. I have been hurt and I have been redeemed. I want to show you Paris, I want to read you a poem. Right now you are asleep and my body instinctively makes the dawn's milk. New Mexico is asleep and the Milky Way shines high.

I am healed between my legs. You are the prettiest human form I have ever seen. You smile and wriggle and you trust and you suck. You know my body better than I might ever imagine. Since your birth, my body has become something greater than its limits. It has put you into this world. Now I have learned this language and I give its form.

December 1995. Our new family flies from Albuquerque to Cleveland. The layover in Saint Louis turns into a delay. Baby Claire has an ear infection. My husband and I sit on the floor in the St. Louis airport, our backs against the rows of seats, the overpacked diaper bag next to our feet. The baby's schedule is getting ruined by time changes and flights in the air. I am going to get used to this. We administer the pink amoxycillin to her through a syringe— we drip the syrupy medicine into her open mouth, like that of a bird that has lost its mother. She nurses. The delay turns into a cancelled flight, an overnight stay. We are transported to our hotel, compliments of the airline.

It is midnight. New parents, we have no idea what to do. The baby wriggles and squeals on the forlorn hotel bed. She has complete trust in us. I am more tired than I thought would be possible. I am getting used to this as well. After we all wriggle and look around us at the hotel room and giggle, we sleep.

We spend Christmas at my parents' house, sleeping in my childhood bedroom. It is freezing outside and my bedroom does not hold the heat too well. I had forgotten the cold and the snow. The snow falls harder and harder, covering the lilac tree in its frozen stance, the one by the side of the house, close to the little door where the milk would be delivered in glass bottles, frozen in winter, with creased foil caps.

I check on my baby girl on and off through the night, in the cold bedroom where I slept from the ages of nine to eighteen, the room where I arranged stuffed animals, where I wrote my college application essays, the room where I starved myself, becoming a light, blue-eyed spirit —130 pounds, 125, 120, 115. Now I am sleeping in this room with my husband and first child. The baby's body is so vulnerable, legs tucked under bottom, beautiful head turned to one side, the infant profile emphasizing the strong fragility of the cranium, nape of neck with downy hair, the human mind and the darling human form.

We then fly to Chicago. A fancy hotel. I interview for jobs. Assistant professor of French.

We return to New Mexico. Baby Claire clings to us in complete trust. Sleep, nurse, be held and bathed, play.

The spring winds come to New Mexico. A steady howl for weeks. Clouds of dirt billowing through the air. Tumbleweeds. Pieces of juniper in flight. The electric smell of lightning. The baby in my arms. The baby at my breast. The baby on my hip. The baby on my back.

She won't nap. Hardly ever. I walk with her in a backpack on my back. I have lost a bit of weight from the exertion of carrying her growing form. I cook with her in the backpack on my back—blue nylon fabric and an aluminum frame. She peers over my left shoulder while I stir or chop, over my right shoulder while I read the recipe. She is intent on understanding what I am doing. There are few sounds except for her breathing, my breathing, the utensils stirring in the steam, the moan of the desert wind outside. Suddenly her soft head is heavy against my back and shoulder. Her nap. Soon her daddy will be home.

I get a phone call from Agnes Scott College in Atlanta, Georgia. Could I come for a campus interview? First I must be interviewed in French on the phone. My husband comes home and plays with the baby while I am interviewed on a long-distance call. I explain, in French, what I am interested in teaching, the texts I might use, the research I want to pursue. I am invited to campus.

I leave my new baby for the first time in order to interview for this tenure-track job. A friend takes me to the airport at dawn. Racing north to Albuquerque in the new light of the desert, I cry steadily upon leaving her. He is a good friend and I feel safe crying in front of him.

There is still milk in my breasts when I leave her, although I have all but stopped nursing her.

Today as I write this, in 2002, it has been almost three years since I have nursed my second baby. And there are still drops of milk in my breasts.

I fly to Atlanta, meet the dean, teach a model class, drink punch and eat a cookie. Even during the initial interview, the dean mentions something about my weight. She compares her own slender form to mine, perceiving in it a mark of discipline, high achievement, priority, control. I interview wearing a black skirt with ribbons on the side, an item I bought secondhand in Paris as a student. I matched it to a blouse also purchased secondhand.

I teach Baudelaire for the model class. Outside, snow begins to fall on the campus. This is highly unusual for Georgia. As I teach the poetry, situating Baudelaire in the context of romanticism and symbolism, engaging the students whom I have never met, three professors observe me.

I am taken out to dinner at a French restaurant. I sleep in a suite in a dorm. I am given meal tickets for cafeteria breakfasts. Alone, in the morning, eating buttery grits and drinking coffee, I look out the windows of the small campus cafeteria. The magnolia trees are regal and stately in their gentle repose. Their leaves are soft and still and slow, like the voices of the women who served my breakfast. Outside, the slow whistle and chug of a train. The train cars marked "Southern." I want this job.

I shake hands with the department chair and go out to the airport. I fly back to the desert with its wild open embrace, to my husband with his strong warm embrace, to my baby girl with her tiny embrace. I have been away from her for two days.

A few days later, the telephone rings. It is the dean. I am offered the job.

My husband has been offered two or three postdoctoral fellowships, but none is in Atlanta. His positions are tempting but temporary. After two or three years, we would need to move and find new work. My offer is potentially long-term. We decide to follow my job offer. We decide that Atlanta is big enough that he will be able to find work in his field too.

The college will pay for our move back east. We are going to leave the desert, the jags of light in the red skies, the stacked enchiladas and Mexican beer, the mesas that transform your mind in the light.

Our desert baby girl will not remember her first year of life spent in the Southwest. But we will visit and show her pictures and tell her, "This is where you were born." Something inside her will always speak of the vast space, the light in her eyes, the heat, the color, the freedom and its vulnerability.

The wedding china is again packed away. I have lost

track of where my wedding dress is. My mother tells me it is in the family home. The books, the tiny clothes, the table and chairs—packed up and moved.

In the abandoned desert my body opened in pain and blood to let the life come. I encountered the meaning of my life in a woman's body in that surrender to another, to blood, to milk, to red light, to blue light. I experienced the mystery of birth, traced always resolutely along a horizon of death.

This was a new kind of poetry, of thinking, of feeling. It was human individuality swallowed up in a desert sky. It was one newborn girl riding in a car seat while her nervous first-time parents gazed upon a lone tree. It was bathing her for the first time, in the sink of a rented apartment, while the wind howled and moaned outside, a reminder of nature's clutch in the face of human helplessness. It was falling in love, the kind of love that goes beyond the body, the kind that would lay the body down for the sake of the other, my form sacrificed for her breath, the beat of her heart, her tiny suck of warm milk in the middle of the night.

This was a falling in love against a canvas of light, her toes, her eyes, framed by violet evening, love felt within the smell of crackling light, electricity in the air, the expanse of mesa and sky that empty the mind of thought and quicken the beat of the heart.

This was sacrifice, sleeplessness, and pain. This was the desert offering no reply to my repeated questions. No museum, no café, no teacher or book to guide me through the labyrinth of my thoughts. No tickets to the exhibition, no café-crème served on a marble table. This was a brute limit, a coming to terms with my physical life. Running on the mesas with rocks in my hands to ward off wild dogs. Swimming under a sun so hot it turned my skin several shades darker in a half hour. Drinking water out of elemental thirst, water without which you would die. Finding shade as pure survival, utter protection.

New Mexico taught me that I could push a child out of my womb with almost no pain relief. I could write two hundred pages on French literature. I could speed along the highway, pregnant, at speeds unknown in the East or Midwest. The desert taught me what it feels like to be the only one on that road, in red light, in an arid ninety-five degrees, with no cell phone, and a different sort of miles to go before I sleep.

New Mexico is random and wild.

The heat of the desert, the vastness, the death of its life. The beauty that comes from such inhospitable solitude.

I resisted it for many months while I was there. Now I miss it almost every day.

Salamanders gliding to and fro in baking heat. A pregnant woman stepping into a clear turquoise pool.

A mother and her infant joined together in the flow of warm milk.

The two together, and the young, strong man, packing their books and bone china, the delicate china with the meandering fruit, to move together to a new city, new jobs, another baby yet to come.

The desert has no care for any of this.

Red light, pink light, violet light, deepest blue.

Red or green chile?

Wedges of lime with Mexican beer.

The salt on the corn chips combined with the ice water, not a taste to stave off mild hunger but sustenance for survival in a deadly heat.

The plane lifts off and disappears into a solid blue sky, a silver afterthought above barren land.

Leaving. Driving through that light, under that light, in that light.

The desert a struggle that has now become my craving,

The hard message of that sky—

Wild cradle of light—

    romance of indifference,

        fragmented lullaby of light

           this inhibition

              Adios

                Au revoir

                  Bye bye

Atlanta

The New Mexico desert opened me up fearfully by forcing me to see. Out there you cannot hide; you see in all directions for hundreds of miles. Georgia both closes me and opens me through what it does not show. Atlanta is a maze of roads and trees. At times here you cannot see fifty feet ahead.

The desert laid itself bare for me, a blank canvas for me to see and to read. In Georgia, the florid vegetation offers a different kind of text—complicated, alive, growing, thriving. The desert was the page. These southern leaves and blooms resemble calligraphy.

We move to Decatur, a self-contained urban-suburban city within the metro perimeter of Atlanta. We rent a college house, sight unseen. The first night there we sleep on the floor with our ten-month-old daughter near us in a portable nylon crib. We are all exhausted. The next morning I am awakened by her frightened, desperate cry. She has awakened early and is completely disoriented. The house is empty and we will wait for the furniture for two days. I sit on the floor in the empty house to give the baby a bottle.

On the second night after we move to Atlanta with our first daughter, my husband and I take her in the stroller on a warm June evening to begin to learn the neighborhood streets.

We stroll down the length of Adams Street. Leaves and flowering bushes grow shoulder high and hang down in front of our heads. The foliage is so thick that we have to push it aside with our hands in order to continue down the sidewalk. My hands grip the navy blue handle of the stroller. My husband's hands are strong and beautiful as he pushes aside the deep green. Lush, moist leaves move secretively in a subtle breeze. Sunlight filters through the spaces in between. The sidewalk is cracked into pieces in places. The world is calm. This street is genteel. There are certainly secrets in these leaves and in the shadows that this green casts.

At our first address, the backyard was lovely—unbelievably deep and green.

The profusion overwhelmed me. I have never been a gardener and I was bewildered by the dense growth. Kudzu wound its way prolifically, insidiously, over the bushes in the recesses of the backyard. My husband valiantly pulled it away. Within two weeks it had covered the same area again with its thriving dark green hood.

Near the back door there was a small hydrangea bush.

It was rapidly getting strangled by choke weed. At first I did not notice the entanglement of translucent green weed and iridescent blue-purple bloom. Then I drew closer and saw that the hydrangea was being fiercely choked by the weed. I stood knee deep in groundcover and pulled long strings of weed out of the bush. The more I grasped, the more the twisted weed came forth, as if the act of my reaching caused further growth. I could not free the hydrangea of it all. The weeds were too fast for me. My gloved fingers could not keep up with them. Inside, my baby girl was waiting to be fed.

If I tugged too hard at the weeds, they destroyed the delicate hydrangea as they became disentangled. I had to unwind the weeds gently from the pale blooms and stems. At times I was too forceful. The act of removing the weeds tore out a fragile sphere of flower. The bloom fell onto the huge pile of weed, a stain of variegated blue against a mound of solid green.

As we discover the backyard, the rooms of the house, the closet space, and the trees and sky, we simultaneously unpack boxes. My childhood poems and photos stay sealed in their cardboard box taped up and labeled "J childhood" in magic marker scrawl.

Boxes of clothes for all seasons. The wedding china so carefully wrapped. Heavy books. Photos and jewelry. Coffee mugs and oriental rugs. The undergraduate papers I wrote on T. S. Eliot and French women writers. The pink journal from high school in which I wrote my spare lists of food consumed.

Alongside the cardboard boxes is another box, one that does not exist in physical space. My body and my mind go in and out of it. It is weightless and transparent and it is where I went for a very long time.

During this time, and for the next several years, it is

as if I am enclosed in a box of glass, a transparent noth-ingness, clear and light, with clean edges unseen.

No one could tell that I was inside that box of glass. Not even me.

The birth of my second daughter, clinical depression, psychoanalysis, and this writing have allowed me—or per-haps forced me—to break its walls.

The box of glass was a box of emptiness—nonbeing, nonfeeling—avoiding, playing hide-and-seek in my mind. It was not asking myself questions. It was not noticing my own intelligence, my own beauty. It was a stillness that resisted the fullness of growth.

I was afraid to break out of it. I was inside its frames —a form of stillness—and to emerge meant destroying the clear panes, the neat edges, the soundlessness of its perfection. To step out of it is truly to enter into this life, this place, this city, its streets and its people and all of this green. To emerge from it means to stop fearing my own strength and my own emotions, to remove the weeds in order to cultivate the beauty they were trying to destroy.

Breaking out of it has hurt so much. Remaining within its stasis was hurting even more.

The glass box kept me at a safe distance from myself. A clarity more pure for being remote. A way for me to think and feel through transparent separation.

The mind seeks this safety at great cost. The cost is soli-tude and fear and awful loneliness. I am trying to leave this clear frame behind—the imprint of wings traced in fresh snow against a dark night.

In a mind of glass there is no mistake, no shadow, nothing opaque. There is no risk. Yet there is an emptiness and a silence that can turn your heart cold.

Now I am writing about the present. The steady grind of a train moving through Decatur, where I live. Six years of hard work as an assistant professor rewarded by tenure at the college where I teach. Most importantly, my second child.

Writing about the present is a confrontation with the weeds. It is the moment of unraveling their twisted stems from gentler blooms. Like the choke weed behind our first rented house, I cannot keep up with the present. I find an hour, two hours, during which to write this, here, in a room of my own, with my little bit of money, as I listen to the song of the spring birds being eclipsed by a sudden, urban siren.

Outside now, right now, dawn is filtering through the huge stands of trees. The street is quiet. My family is asleep. The leaves sway gently in a May breeze. Blue sky and cloud, flicker of bird and light.

This writing of the present is bound to be less stable. I cannot see. My touch is tentative. I am so afraid. This virgin loneliness is without end.

This confrontation with fear and instability represents my emerging from the box of glass. Tentatively. Desperately.

Emerging to cling to the beauty of my life—my work, my body, my family, this city—no longer to hide from its complexity and sorrow.

To feel anger, resentment, elation, surprise. To find a new friend and explore—after so long—what that feels like. What it feels like to get close. Not to be inside a wall of glass. To wear high heels and trust the risk of lipstick. To be the woman I have become—a mother, a writer, someone who can love profoundly and be deeply loved.

Getting outside of a mind made of glass means breaking the transparency, the pristine separation. It means leaving dirty dishes in the sink and clothes on the floor in order to walk outside and feel the evening air. Letting my daughters fight and make forts with the living room furniture. Reading to my older daughter deep into the evening and putting aside my writing to work the "Whose Mother?" photo-puzzle with my toddler. It means constant interruption and mess; it means terrible difficulty and the fleeting beauty I want to capture in these words.

It means never fully knowing and understanding this limitation. Drawing ever nearer while being ever deprived of the perfect word or touch. The success of each day's failures and the empty failure of perfection's success.

&

In the summer of 1996, my husband and baby daughter and I began to claim an existence in the largest city in the South in a summer during which it hosted the Olympic games. Olympic village, skyrocketing real estate prices, local politics, and international energy. I began to go to my new office every day, the same office I have now, on the third floor of one of the main buildings on campus. Above the west door where I often enter are stone carvings of a palette and paintbrush, a book and a pen. I seldom forget that they are there, the stasis of comfort that they provide.

There is a vast oak tree outside the two tall windows in my office on campus. It has come to offer me comfort over the twelve semesters that I have been here. Its leaves brush and flirt green against the panes of glass. In autumn they form a concert of color and then fall in cascades before my eyes. I have watched the branches whip across each other in sudden summer storms and I have been surprised six times by the emergence of growth each spring.

During the summer of 1996 I start going to my office to prepare for my first semester. One colleague who has been assigned to be my faculty mentor takes me out to lunch nearby. Another colleague sees me coming and going every day and barely musters any conversation beyond hello.

I take my daughter on strolls around our new surroundings. She has learned to walk early—ten and a half months—but spends another few months holding on to one of my fingers. My light touch assures her body of its balance and strength although it does not provide any real physical support. She is plump and blue-eyed and curious and gorgeous. One day we walk onto the south side of campus and I sit her down momentarily on the grass. I have no idea about fire ants in Georgia—the mound of sand that hides their teeming mass. I place her inadvertently upon such a mound. Within one or two minutes she starts to wail. I pick her up and see red welts spotting her little perfect dimpled thighs. I hurry home with her, feeling inadequate and awful. My husband and I treat the bites with hydrocortisone cream. Later that day she has her one-year portrait taken wearing a tiny sundress and white tights to hide the bites.

One night late in that first summer my husband and I were watching the Olympic games. In the shadow of the galley kitchen of our rented house, my husband saw a dark shape run past. He told me it was a mouse but he knew it was a rat. Rats had been crisscrossing our kitchen floor during the night for weeks, in a house in which our infant child slept.

We called the college maintenance office the next morning immediately at 8 a.m. It was a Friday. They asked if "it" could wait until Monday. We said absolutely not. When the employees from the physical plant came to check, I had our daughter on my left hip and was in a state of near hysteria. I stood ten inches away from the men during the entire time that they checked our house. There was an open space from our dirt basement that led directly into the kitchen. With my baby on my hip, her little legs dangling on either side of my hips and her hands on my shoulders, I pointed my finger into every corner and commanded that they get down on their knees and check every square inch of space.

They set a few traps in the kitchen. That night I barely slept at all. I wanted to take our baby in my arms and flee. In the morning after fragmented sleep, my husband braved the kitchen and disposed of the trapped, dead rat.

How was I ever to make sense of this place?

&

When I work intensely—in a tenure-track teaching job, on this book—I step back into the box of glass. Pure thought, perfect concentration, unsullied by the time and mess required by the consumption of food. The time, the mess, the fear, and the confusion. I must remind myself to drink and to eat. It is still hard. The mind does not want to be reined in by flesh and blood.

The desert had turned its vast page to me in a spare writing of juniper and light. Lightning jagged against vast red. A purple storm seventy miles away. A clean edge of death in the line between sun and shade.

Georgia offers such different configurations in its natural writing of life and death. Magnolia blooms falling open for months, their vast petals of perfume hanging in moist July air. The white spread of their flower seems so impossible; how can it lie so open among the leaves, suspended there in the moment before the petal falls?

Cockroaches darting across the kitchen floor—red-brown, hairy legs, making me want to gasp for air.

The crepe myrtle—in stillness again, suspended in oppressive humidity in mid-July, its deep pink-red blooms cone-shaped and referring to absolutely nothing beyond themselves.

The garish azaleas in springtime—a thousand bright little ladies in bright little skirts, trumpeting color across the entire city in row upon row, deep pink and white, light pink and white, the cultivated domestic type and the indigenous, wilder, and more vulnerable kind.

The leaves that form canopies over residential streets, the green that grows steadily toward home and street. Lamplight is required in midsummer because the green is so dense that the rooms inside become dark.

Thin Again.

My weight dips below 130 pounds during my first year as a tenure-track assistant professor of French.

I begin to lose my way in the intensity of my work. I talk to a therapist once a week. She is young—maybe younger than I—and totally composed and apart. She asks me how I feel about coming to the appointment. I am not sure how to respond. She does not even begin to coax me out of my box of glass. It is going to be years before the right therapist—a psychiatrist and analyst—will find the way to do that.

She asks me to stand and turn around so she can look at me. I obey and suffer a wave of intense self-consciousness and shame. It has taken me until now—in the moment of this writing—even to realize how I felt.

As the months go on I notice her body starting to change and realize that she is with child. I know before she tells me. She is wearing maternity clothes before she does. When she tells me I tell her I already knew. I am good at observing from behind my clear pane. She tells me that she will continue only for a while longer, that because of her first child our therapy will need to come to an end. This is a ghost transference of my mother who is pregnant with my younger sister. I know this deep down but do not really explore it. She asks me if I have any questions. I ask her if she knows the sex. She tells me she will be having a girl. At the end of our last session she reaches to me in a hug. Loss chokes my heart like a wild weed.

A new period of instability begins. At work I progress steadily toward tenure. In my first year my doctoral dissertation is accepted for publication. I strive to get my bearings on campus, with colleagues, in the classroom. I teach an upper-level course on the French Enlightenment with nineteen students enrolled.

During this time, I sacrifice part of my thoughts and feelings to the glass box. Inadvertently I slip back into its enclosed transparency, the clarity of its illusions. My body is light and clear and does not weigh me down or hold me back. My mind is untethered by the weight of form.

The oak tree outside my window loses its leaves in November and pushes forth tender new leaves in April. I am nearing the end of my first year as a new professor. I am making my way professionally. Emotionally I am losing ground. I am in a prolonged relapse and I do not even notice. My weight hovers in the upper 120s—lower than the low point of the recommended weight for my height. I weigh just enough to continue menstruating. Once or twice I see a photograph and think that I look slim. A friend at church mentions something about my weight. I do not know how to hear her. I care for my daughter, my husband, my students.

November 1997. Thanksgiving day. A new journey begins in my body. While our first daughter naps before friends come to dine, we conceive our second daughter. Outside the leaves crisp and color turns. There is a chilly breeze. With our friends and our daughter, we eat and visit. I enjoy a glass of red wine. Inside my body a fat ovum is being penetrated by one spearheaded sperm.

Our second daughter came to us as a force of nature. She was conceived during the only time in which we did not prevent pregnancy. The one-time chance for conception is statistically around one in one thousand.

Something deep inside me knew that I would conceive. My slim body was about to wrap itself around a new life, grow round and large again, give birth again, nurse again. I was going to have to break the box of glass and move through warm milk and blood and thousands of tears.

That winter I was scheduled to lead a group of students to France and Switzerland through an academic study program called Global Connections. Two weeks before Christmas I took the pregnancy test. It was somewhat early for the result to show, yet I observed the telltale blue line, a new kind of writing in and of my body, the elusive sign that I was again with child.

How was I going to lead an international trip while my body was in the throes of a new pregnancy? How would I be able to give birth again while working toward tenure? My body began to show me the way. This pregnancy and this birth were going to break me down in order to build me back up, differently, in more fragility and more strength. Somehow I was going to find the way to do this.

Aching, terribly tender breasts. Map of deep blue veins on their expanding surface. Ouch. Bathing our toddler while waves of nausea swept over me. Christmas. My parents visit. Although we are vegetarian, they want to have turkey. My mother roasts a turkey breast in our oven and the odor nauseates me horribly. After Christmas my mother takes me shopping to buy me a winter coat for the trip to Europe. In the department store, among the wool coats and display lights, I begin to feel faint. My mother helps me sit down, finds me a drink.

In my womb the cells are dividing, differentiating into heart and brain, eye buds and finger buds. Forming a tiny spine, a tiny liver, tiny toes, the female sex.

My parents return home to Cleveland. I have morning sickness in the late afternoon. Morning sickness is a misnomer. I feel best in the morning. My husband takes me out for my birthday to a restaurant in Buckhead. I sit waiting for the food to come in a state of sweating nausea. The minute we get home I head back to our bathroom and get sick. The skin around my eyes is a mask of broken blood vessels—fragile purple in color—from the vomiting.

Saltines. Soda water. If I move even slightly, the nausea washes over and through me as if I am adrift in open sea.

Mid-January 1998. It is time to take nine students to Europe on an academic trip. I am the only faculty leader.

I cry and cry upon leaving Claire. I will be gone two weeks. I pray that I will be physically able to do this. The plane lifts into the air. Inside my body my second daughter continues to form, safe and sound in my enclosed warmth.

Paris. This city, this language I adore. White sheets and gray rooftops. The excitement and the responsibility at hand actually eclipse the nausea and the fatigue. A few of my students—French majors—are seeing Paris for the first time. We are blessed with unusually warm, sunny weather —sixty-five degrees in January for the entire week in Paris. I manage to feel okay. I lead the group through various parts of the city. One student complains continually that she is tired. I offer her a Mona Lisa smile in response. Then I forge ahead, six weeks pregnant, leading the group like a mother duck with her ducklings in tow.

A few days into the trip I reveal to the group that I am expecting. The students are considerate and sweet. But I remain apart, my mind behind a pane of glass. I do not allow myself to get close to them. That is one way in which I am able to cope. It will be a while before I allow myself to get close to a student. On this trip I am ultimately re-mote.

There is a recent Agnes Scott graduate on the trip who serves as my assistant. For two of the evening events I ask her to accompany the group. I cannot continue late into the night. She takes the students to the concert, the play, and I curl up in my hotel room near the Louvre to read. I read Annie Ernaux—*Une Femme*. It describes the author caring for her mother at the end of her mother's life. If I lie still and read in the quiet of my *chambre*, I can enter into this language, these words, while my body creates my tiny girl inside.

I travel with my students from Paris to Geneva, Switzerland. Our study tour continues: The Institut Voltaire in Geneva at his former home, Les Délices. The Musée Rousseau at the University of Geneva. The romantic town of Annecy where Rousseau first laid eyes on his deep love, Madame de Warens, whom he called *Maman*.

I stave off the nausea and the fatigue by eating what I can of the meals that are placed before me. I marvel at my students' first encounter with immersion in French.

Together, we peer at manuscript editions of Rousseau's work and letters in Voltaire's hand. We sip some champagne at the top of the Eiffel Tower. We buy souvenirs and trinkets and books.

At the end of the trip my body starts to give in to the strain. In Geneva we are lodged in a noisy hotel near the train station. During the last few nights my homesickness for my toddler overwhelms me with grief. I cry and give in to the stress alone. The "morning" sickness returns in the evenings. I get sick in my hotel room, then stagger over to my suitcases to pack. It has gotten cold now. I clutch a warm sweater and wrap it around me.

We return to Atlanta. I am nearly mad with the desire to see Claire. She is waiting for me with my husband in the airport. To my relief and delight she comes right into my arms.

I return on my birthday. I can barely lift a fork to my mouth. I am worn out and nauseated from the first trimester.

Classes begin again. I am still in the early weeks of the pregnancy and still feeling exhausted. One day I get sick on the quad, in public, on my way to my office. No one sees me, yet I am appalled. It is about 8 a.m. I have no idea how to continue. I go to the ladies' room and clean my mouth. I then go to my office and call my husband. By this time he too is on tenure-track at the same college. This is going to prove stressful for us both, but it is not the kind of job offer to turn down. I tell him I do not know how I'm going to do this—stay on tenure-track, take care of my first child, give birth to this child. He reassures me. We can make it, he says. It will be okay.

In a few weeks, it begins to be okay. But only in a physical sense. My body settles into the second trimester. The fetus inside is formed—delicate spine, curve of tiny finger, swimming, floating, moving in the ocean womb. I pray again for a girl.

Emotionally, something is starting to go wrong. The anxiety is rendering me less stable. At the movies with my husband in a large, fancy mall, I stand still in a frozen panic, utterly bewildered as to how to purchase the tickets. I am like a column of salt. I cannot take the escalator. I cannot move. My husband tells me to wait. He runs to buy the tickets. When he returns, my panic has passed. I take his arm and we go into the movie. We both try to pretend there is nothing to worry about. Inside, the flower of my mind—blue hydrangea—is starting to be choked by weeds of insecurity, anxiety, depression.

I keep teaching. Once a month, I climb into our little car and drive for my prenatal appointment. Each time I get weighed. My weight climbs through the 130s, 140s, and 150s. My older sister counsels me to stop paying attention, not to look at the scale when I am weighed during medical visits. This pregnancy is more demanding. I am working full-time and I already have one child. There are no more naps. And my body wants more food.

During one prenatal visit the nurse scolds me for gaining too much weight. I have taken my sister's advice and have stopped looking at the numbers. By the time I meet with my midwife I am almost in tears. I explain to her that the nurse criticized my weight gain. I explain to the midwife that I have a history of anorexia.

Fourteen years after the deep center of the anorexia, I am only just beginning to say the word out loud. I have never talked about this before.

The midwife is patient and reassuring. She tells me the nurse should not have criticized me. She asks me to tell her the nurse's name. I tell her I cannot remember.

A few weeks later I return for the ultrasound. I am alone. My husband either has to work or take care of Claire. There will be many moments of solitude during this pregnancy, giving birth to this child.

"You'll feel some warm goop," the technician tells me. I remember this from before. Squirt. Her implement (what is it called?) squishes into the "goop" and begins to travel around the small mound of my tummy. One side, another, over the surface it moves. The fetus is asleep. The technician wants the fetus to wake up so that she can get a better indication of heart rate and movement. She takes some kind of contraption that produces a loud snap of sound, loud enough to travel through the warm amniotic fluid of my womb. The little form moves more quickly, perhaps startled. I feel so protective. What a shame to be startled awake while still in the womb.

The technician tells me it is a girl. I look out the window to the blue outside while a smile spreads across my face. I am thrilled. Claire will have a sister.

February. March. April. Spring comes to Georgia. Pale green leaves and thousands of azaleas. The baby moving and squirming inside. I sense differences between the two pregnancies, between the two babies. This baby sleeps more inside my body. As I write this today, she still requires more sleep. During my pregnancy with her I feel her fingers down at the bottom of my womb, stroking gently, sweeping softly. She still does that gesture with her fingers now—across her daddy's back and with her pink baby blanket.

I teach my classes. When I begin to get quite round I tell them I'm going to have a baby. The students are eager and proud and kind. I talk to Claire about her little sister inside me. She begins to refer to the baby as "her" baby. We talk about names. We think a lot about Madeleine.

When we ponder other names, Claire, who is only two and a half, protests: "No, my baby is Madeleine!" We decide to name her Madeleine Marie.

My dissertation is published in book form. Spring is blooming and my body has settled into carrying another life. I reach a kind of shaky harmony. It is not going to last.

Sometimes, at the blackboard when I turn my back briefly to the class while preparing to write something in chalk, I panic. Anxiety is starting to creep in and take over. Work, marriage, one child, and pregnant. Teaching, research, service: the three areas of accomplishment one needs to prove for tenure.

Growing up, my mother would sometimes serve dinner, go into the kitchen to remove her apron, come back to her seat, sit down, look at my father, my sisters, and me with a cool gaze, and announce, "I cannot breathe." Anxiety used to shut her windpipe closed. Somehow she would get through it. No one knew what to say.

Now I was starting to understand the grip of anxiety, a feeling of imbalance taking hold, a weed winding its way around my throat. Responsibilities were growing wild in my life and I still had not gotten past a psychiatric illness that claims the lives of many sufferers.

If I wanted to be a mother who could reach and grasp all the contours of her heart, I would need to process the anorexia nervosa that I had suffered—what it had meant, why it had happened, why it still came back now. But I did not. My therapist had left to have her baby. She and I had barely begun when it was time for her to go. Now my second child swelled my form and mildly kicked and slumbered inside.

Summer. The hottest summer on record in Atlanta for many, many years. Potato chips. Lemonade. Cheese. Pasta.

This baby requires more food than Claire did. My weight goes up above 170. I am partly aghast and partly resigned. The baby comes first. One of my pregnancy books lists exercises to be done within hours of giving birth. Simple leg lifts to start a process of toning that can lead to the loss of pregnancy weight. How can it be that we live in a culture where, until very recently, women returned home within twenty-four hours of giving birth? How can it be that women still return home before their milk has come in, before they are healed, and yet they are still advised in writing about leg lifts and Kegel exercises to help them "shed pregnancy pounds?" What is this fear of the female body? What is the origin of our lust for its minimal form? Why can't I shake it, embrace fat round curves, rolls of flesh, the fertile fecundity? In truth I am still terrified of fat.

At work, at church, I am told that I "do not even look pregnant." I hear this repeatedly and it is meant as a compliment. Yet it creates rather the opposite effect. This so-called flattery negates my body, eclipses the art and the work that it is doing. How am I to feel about "not even looking pregnant"? The privacy of my body seems laid bare for the words of others. Because of this claim placed on my body by others, its intimacy seems more removed from my authority.

At my checkups my belly is measured with a yellow centimeter tape. Toward the end of the pregnancy the midwife begins to put her fingers inside me to check for dilation and effacement. This body vocabulary, words for an expectant mother, enters my mindset again. How many centimeters have I opened? Am I effaced—thin—or shut tight and thick? I talk to the midwife about my previous birth, the pain, the fear, the not knowing and the induction. My mother's labors were exactly like this.

I am at a new point in my body story. Ahead of me lies more sorrow than I can possibly imagine. The weeds encircle the fresh blooms and I cannot see to tear them away. My concentration is on my toddler and the new baby inside.

I could not know all that lay ahead of me. A crushing blow of postpartum depression. Rapid weight loss. Clinical anxiety. Medication. Therapy. Psychoanalysis. And through psychoanalysis, the ability to write, to write this story, to hear my fingers flying over these keys, in peace. As I write this, my two daughters are slumbering peacefully upstairs in their twin beds, on clean cotton sheets. Their light eyelashes lie in lush, straight rows while their steady hearts beat in time to their breath.

Now it is their time to live the innocence of the girl body, with its speed and movement and agile grace. Now they travel through the body's childhood garden and I watch in admiration. They are pure bloom with no weeds —hydrangea, magnolia, white azalea, pink azalea—fragrant, everlasting in the moment of their own passing in between shadows and leaves.

August 1998. I am sleeping in the front room of our first rented house, the house where the rats crept across the kitchen at night. All of the holes have been stopped up for years—the holes leading from the dirt basement of that bungalow. I am at term with my second baby and I need to have an entire bed to myself—like a mare who finds an empty stall in a barn. I turn from one side to another, slowly, slowly. Our first daughter sleeps in the room adjacent to this front room. I am comforted to know she is so close by. My husband sleeps alone in the back of the house, in our room that is connected to the little nursery we have prepared.

Outside, in the early morning, city buses roll past the front of the house. In the evenings the cicadas moan their late summer song. The heat and sun are intense and the

Giving Birth

air is thick with humid vapor. In the backyard, the kudzu winds its way insidiously, in thick twines, around bushes and up the trunks of trees.

I have Braxton-Hicks contractions: my womb bunches up in places into a baseball. The vast muscle is remembering how to give birth, how to contract and push the baby through the birth canal. My thoughts have no part in this process. This is pure body, pure physical life. My body as center and creator of life has no true relation to the workings of my mind.

My midwife agrees that I am ready. I am going to be induced again. My body is opening, thinning out. At Northside Hospital in Atlanta—nicknamed "the baby factory" due to the high annual numbers of births—all of the beds are full. I joke that it must be the full moon. I am waiting for a bed in which to give birth. As soon as a bed becomes available I will be called to come.

August 8. Sunday. The phone rings at 9 a.m. A bed is free. My husband has taken Claire to church already. I will not have the chance to say goodbye to her, to tell her Mommy is going to the hospital for her baby sister to come out. I weep for her as I throw a few things into my hospital bag, grieving for the lost chance to hug her and say bye bye.

Our close friend will pick Claire up from church and care for her for as long as necessary. My husband and I take her the key to our house. We drive the empty streets of Atlanta, curve around the rare quiet of I-285 and head north to the hospital. We sit and wait. Fill out papers.

Then they are ready for me. I do not remember the preliminary hours. I remember the hospital gown, white with blue design, and the cotton ticking cloth of the almost useless ties. IV—sharp silver needle piercing the vein in my hand. Once again I will be given Pitocin. Once again the hook-like implement pierces the membranes that hold amniotic fluid. This is partly my choice. I could have stayed on, waiting while my womb bunched in hard baseballs of muscle, not sleeping, not sleeping in the same bed with my husband, lying up at night listening to the cicadas and imagining the child inside. Instead I have asked the midwife to let me enter, now, into the act of giving birth.

I am lucky and receive a very nice birthing room with lamplight and floral furniture. A private room. The Pitocin starts its work. This time there are no complications. The baby's rate is monitored on one screen while another screen shows the intensity of each contraction. My midwife, whose name is Dixie, checks inside me. She tells me she is going to open me more with her fingers—"rough me up" is the phrase she uses to describe the medical process of stripping my membranes. I have felt this kind of thing before. It does not hurt.

Blood pressure. Fetal heart rate. Pitocin dripping in one drop at a time. I am getting the epidural this time. After a few hard, painful contractions, the midwife calls for the anesthesiologist to come. For this birth I receive consistent medical attention and care. Dixie is cheerful and red-haired, a midwife who does not preach any particular type of birth, a woman who wants to care for other women as they give birth, whether they choose an unmedicated or a medicated labor.

Epidural. I need to sit on the edge of the hospital bed and curl my spine in a fetal pose and hold perfectly still. I cry a little bit. I am ambivalent about accepting the anesthesia. In part I wish I could forego it. This is the tyranny of "being strong," waiving the pain relief. But I have experienced the true pain of labor and this time I want to eclipse it. The anesthesiologist locates the precise lumbar space between two vertebrae in my spine. I hold my breath

Giving Birth

while the needle goes in. Prick, glide, deep inside. Then the nurse helps me lie back in bed on my left side.

Within twenty minutes, the pain of the contractions is completely gone. My husband watches the monitor as it shows wavy parabolas of the pain I do not feel. My womb is contracting in its entirety, pushing the baby deeper through me, in me, beyond me. My husband asks, "Did you feel anything? That was a huge contraction." "Nope," I say. This is the way to go. I watch the mother-baby show on the TV while the monitor wildly records its bell curves of contracting pain. The TV displays images of perfectly groomed mothers nursing their new babies while older siblings look dreamily on.

The nurse tells me I should try to "get some rest" and relax while my body does its little miracle of work. The midwife checks on me every half hour. I feel safe in her care. She is attending to another woman who is having a very tough time laboring. Dixie tends to her, then checks on me, in symmetrical alternation. The other woman has been pushing for hours. Long hard hours of pushing often cause the cervix to swell and this makes it even harder for the baby to come. Dixie is trying to help her avoid a cesarean. They need to try forceps. That doesn't work. Dixie has to pass her off to the obstetrician for a "section."

I rest. It is about 1 p.m. My thoughts drift forever to the baby inside me and to our first daughter who is in the care of our friend. All of my past experiences—my girl body, my virgin body, my starving body—are a part of what my body is going through now. These other selves —the girl who climbed the apple tree, the girl who starved herself to the bone, the woman who walked every mile of Paris—they are present within me, circles within circles, waves of memory and dream. My mind opens and drifts as my body labors. I close my eyes. I turn the volume off on the TV images of infants and their mothers. I converse a bit with the nurse who is tending to me. I ask her if most women get the epidural. She says yes. I ask her what she thinks of that. She tells me she doesn't understand why any woman would voluntarily forego the pain relief in favor of the intense pain.

The monitor shows the wild curves that indicate the opening-wide of my body. At my direction, my husband goes to get a tee-shirt for Claire. The tee-shirt has a picture of a little girl and says "I'm the big sister." The hospital gift shop charges an extravagant amount for it. There is a three-dimensional, grosgrain, polka-dot bow sewn onto the shirt at the top of the girl's hair. Claire needs size extra-small. She is going to turn three eleven days from now.

It is about 3 p.m. I feel a gush onto the sheets. The little ocean that held this little girl for nine months. Blood. Elemental liquid flows in rhythmic spurts onto the bleached and sterilized towels and bed linens. The TV mounted above the bed continues to display its impossible story in a seduction of color. Ten centimeters. Time to push.

Dixie helps me into position to push. She asks my husband to help. Long legs folded in half and pressed back past my pelvis, past a ninety-degree angle with my hips. She takes half a jar of Vaseline and widens me in circles over and over again. She is attempting to prevent a tear. One-Two-Three "Push to Ten." The room is quiet. I am not in pain. I feel calm. My body knows this. This is a profound part of its story. It stores and remembers the act of giving birth. I go completely into the act, my thought disappearing into my mind's eclipse. My husband and the midwife press back gently together, one on each leg. "Push to ten." "Thataway!" Do I want a mirror to see, to watch? No. Am I sure? Yes, I am sure. I want to feel myself giving birth without seeing its representation in mirrored re-flection. I want to feel the real of what my body is doing, feel the awe-inspiring pressure and movement of this baby being born.

In this act I return to myself. In giving life to this baby I give myself away, over, in order to find myself. Lost and found and found again. An act of abandon—birth—that brings a form of peace beyond words.

Here she comes in her perfect form, the dream of her head crowning—I feel it, I do not want to see it, this is another kind of vision, the vision of truest sensation, of this deep push, of knowing who I am through what my body is able to do.

One more push and she is born. Lusty cry. I have never felt so happy. My body opened up like the full moon and pushed her out. No tear, no cut. "Just one little stitch," Dixie says as she administers it, "and I am not even per-fectly sure you need that, but I'm going to do it just in case for this one tiny abrasion."

I get to hold her immediately. I pull up my hospital gown. "Yes, warm skin on skin," Dixie says. The nurse be-side my bed grumbles and complains that this "bonding" gets bloodstains on the mothers' hospital gowns. I hold this tiny girl against my warmth. Tiny curled hands, tiny bottom, tiny perfect toes. Her face looks remarkably like mine. Mine looks like my mother's. I can feel her person-ality in this first instant of holding and beholding. Wry. Brilliant. Vulnerable. Something close to forever, beyond anything now.

She nurses.

Suck-Suck-Pause.

Suck-Suck-Pause.

This trinity of silent, innocent movement. Movement that nurtures, takes in, incorporates, literally making a new body, in *corps*.

Rooming in. If you want to keep your newborn with you, you can choose "rooming in." My husband goes home to spend the night with our first child. Earlier, she has come to see the new baby and has touched her and gazed at her and asked me why my hospital bed looks so funny. I show her the buttons on the side that let me tilt up and back.

A nurse comes and asks me to look at a chart posted at eye level on the wall across from the foot of my bed. It describes pain. The number 1 indicates "no pain." The number 10 indicates "unbearable pain." How would I quantify my pain, she asks? She stands with her clipboard and pen, waiting for my answer. "Between 3 and 4," I say. The anesthesia is wearing off. This second childbirth has been easier. What lies ahead is going to be much harder.

Rooming in means that no nurse attends to the newborn. Nurses attend to the mother—checking blood flow from the birth canal, blood pressure—but the newborn is left in the care of the mother who has just given birth hours before. The alternative to rooming in is to send the newborn to the nursery. There, she will be placed in those infamous rows and wrapped in the recognizable white flannel receiving blanket with the wide blue and narrow pink stripes. She will likely be given tiny sample bottles of formula. I am weak and I want to nurse and see her. I try rooming in.

At around midnight, eight hours after giving birth, I push the button that has someone from the nursery come to my room. I ask about diapering and the care of the stump where the umbilical cord had been cut. "We don't do none of that if you're rooming in. You gotta do it all.

Otherwise we take the baby to the nursery." I try to do it all by myself. But I cannot even stand. On doctor's orders I am not to try to walk yet. I call in another nurse. I start to cry. The postpartum hormone levels have begun their steep dive, the estrogen plummeting lower and lower within the space of a few days. This nurse listens to my concerns. I want to nurse my baby, but I am too tired to do all of this alone. And my husband is home with our first child. This nurse convinces me that I need to rest and that the baby should go to the nursery for a while. She tells me that she is on call all night. She will give the baby one feeding of formula so that I can sleep. Then she will bring her to me to nurse. I cry some more and then I let the nurse take her.

I sleep for six hours straight and wake up feeling much stronger. The same nurse comes in. It is about 5 a.m. She says that my new baby is darling and tells me how many ounces of formula she has drunk. I nurse her. Thick, gold-enrod colostrum that looks like some kind of nectar. I thank the nurse for being patient and listening to me. The nurse tells me the mothers who worry her are the ones who do not worry, who do not ask to see their new babies, who do not buzz the nursery to have the baby brought to their room.

The baby stays with me for a couple of hours and then goes back to the nursery. While she is there, she is given a routine screening test. The on-call pediatrician at North-side Hospital comes in and says, "Well, she did not pass the hearing test. But even if she does not have full hearing, don't worry, she will still speak." He does not preface his news with a word of congratulations on the birth, or a question concerning how I feel or how I have rested. Just the news that her hearing may be impaired. I immediately begin to cry. Inside my body the estrogen continues its steep and rapid plummet. I hear the pediatrician's voice instructing me: she will need to have the hearing test repeated at the age of four weeks, she will need to be examined by a pediatric ENT. He leaves. I call my parents and sob. They reassure me as best they can.

I then call my husband. I do not sob when I tell him this. I called my parents first so that I could sob to them and have more strength in my voice when it came time to call my husband. I do not remember our conversation about the baby's hearing.

A nurse comes in to take me to the bathroom for the first time. She needs me to prove that I can pee. This is crucially important, it turns out, for postpartum women. She asks if I am ready to try. Okay, I say. She helps me walk to the bathroom. When I stand up a warm long gush of blood streams between my legs. I go into the bathroom and pee. When I stand up to try to make it back to the bed, I faint, and because I am so tall the nurse cannot hold me up. She is petite (five foot four inches, perhaps). I am crumpled on the sterile tile floor of my hospital room. I hear the nurse's voice as I come to, calling for aid to get me back into the bed. Two nurses help me stand and walk.

The next twenty-four hours are a blurred rhythm of falling in love with the new baby, nursing her, and crying over the possibility that she may have a hearing deficiency. Was it the fact that I traveled so much in my first trimester? Was it the glass of wine I had two weeks before her birth? My husband and our first daughter come and go. Their visits tire me emotionally and physically. I talk to my dear friend in Chapel Hill, my doctoral advisor. Her voice is attentive and birdlike and I love it and her. I eat the tepid food borne in on plastic trays. Drinks with those straws that are ridged and bend at the top into upside-down letter L's: Longing. Loss. Lust. Lament. The mediocre coffee in the morning tastes good, a sign that I am returning to a day-to-day rhythm in my body. The blood continues to gush between my legs and the nurses continue to take my blood pressure.

We bring the baby home. She is a magnolia flower folded and enclosed but at the same time wide open in the Georgia heat. Her fingers curl over the top of her receiving blanket like the newest leaves of a newer flower. Her eyes and ears hold a beauty never before seen, a language never before heard.

For the next few days I nurse while Claire stands vigil at the arm of my chair. She is enthralled by "her" baby and she is also confused and jealous. We give her a pink and white fabric bassinet so she can take care of a dolly while Mommy takes care of her sister. This works for a little while. People come with cards and gifts and hot covered noodles. The August sun pours in through the back windows where I sit and nurse. As with childbirth, my body remembers nursing from before. The milk comes in a pure white wave, a wave of expression to in-corporate this new girl.

At one point in those early weeks, the baby does not have a bowel movement for almost nine days. I worry. Our regular pediatrician reassures me that with breastfeeding babies, the milk is so pure and adapted to the baby that it sometimes is completely absorbed by the growing infant, producing no waste. My milk literally is becoming the dimples on her thighs and elbows and around the enigma of her smile.

Part of me feels as if I am falling apart. The associations between my thoughts and my body are uneasy, ill-formed. My joints that have loosened during pregnancy are finding their regular spaces and tightening again. My body is settling back into nonpregnant life. I weigh myself after being home for a week. Of the forty pounds I had gained, I have lost only ten. I panic to the point that

I can hardly breathe. Then I move over to look at the new baby and my heart breaks into a mosaic of music and light.

The postpartum depression snuck in steadily. The first sign of it came in the earliest weeks. A tree removal team spent several days removing an immense, dead tree from our backyard, right outside the window where I would sit and nurse. The sound of the sawing and the men working, the thud of the limbs, sent my mind into a place of darkest anxiety. I felt as if my emotions were being sawed clear through. The weeping continued. I had to return to work when Madeleine, my open magnolia bloom, was only seven weeks old. This was after an additional week without pay. The college policy offers six weeks. My body was healed but my emotions were in disarray. I stood in front of my classes full of students I did not know, students who had been instructed by a substitute from Emory who gave them all As.

A pernicious form of clinical depression continued to choke my body and mind. It was a flowering of the same depression that had begun when I was seventeen and starving myself in Cleveland.

The pounds melted off me as I worked and survived on broken sleep. Even after Madeleine began to sleep through the night, at around four months, I tossed and turned half the night. My crying spells continued, taking over like summer storm squalls. I would move through the house in the middle of the night, ghost of a woman, emotions in tatters, watching the baby sleep, watching my husband sleep, watching my first child sleep. Then I would lie down on the living room couch, a wanderer in my own home, and listen to the cars pass by while watching the squares of light and shadow created by the panes of glass.

One late October afternoon I sat in my office trying to grade a set of grammar tests. The oak outside my office teased my thoughts and brushed its orange and yellow foliage against the glass. Inside my head, my thoughts were turning and growing colder like the autumn. A winter of depression was starting to set in. I stared at the papers stacked neatly beneath my gaze. I stared at the pen held by my hand. I looked at the students' handwritten French sentences: *le passé composé, le présent, le futur*. Past, present, and future combining in this moment and bringing me to a moment of absolute stasis. Something was very wrong. I could not concentrate on the grading in front of me. I could not sleep. I had no appetite. I had not laughed or felt joy for months.

Emory Clinic for postpartum mood disorders. Depression inventory survey. I passed with high marks. Disturbed sleep, poor concentration, weepiness, changes in appetite, family history, chronic stress and anxiety. I talked to the doctor. I left his office with the free trial pack of Zoloft and his reassurance that it was perfectly okay to continue breastfeeding. He armed me with the articles he himself had authored showing the exact chemical breakdown of Zoloft in the bloodstream and in the breast milk of the nursing mother. Only slight traces were found to pass into the milk.

Like it or not, I knew I was sick, and had to start taking these enigmatic, elliptical blue pills: 10 mg for a few days, 20 mg for a few days, up and up while my thoughts turn 'round and 'round. The first day that I took the smallest dose, I was with my husband in a shopping center. I felt light-headed. After a few weeks my body adjusted to it.

Things started to get a little bit better. I was able to sleep in my own bed with my husband sleeping to my left. I was able to concentrate again at work and was no longer afflicted by a cold grip of anxiety. My appetite showed no change but my energy level improved.

I go through my midterm review in the tenure process. I submit three large binders containing student evaluations, written statements on teaching and research, examples of publications, sample course materials. My teaching is observed. Committees meet and vote.

I stop nursing Madeleine when she is about five months old. I wish I could nurse longer but this is the rhythm that my body must follow. She does not seem to mind. She lusts for her warm bottles of formula and her dimpled arms reach for them. She learns to sit in the darling tripod fashion—both arms forward, palms flat on the floor, her little bottom the third support for her body. When I return home from work to see her, she is sometimes on her back with her infant "gym" placed where her hands can reach. Sometimes she is lost in the bliss of an afternoon nap. Other times she looks expectantly up at me from her solid tripod position. Her smile is a wonderful, spread-open bloom.

It turns out that her hearing is perfect. I take her to the pediatrician and to the pediatric ENT. They poke her and look into her ears. I have to help hold her down, screaming, while they shine the pinpoint of light into her tiny ear canals. She has chronic ear infections during her first year of life, but her hearing is fine. She goes on and off antibiotics. Just as the pediatrician begins to talk seriously about inserting tubes to prevent further infections, they mercifully disappear.

The four of us—Mommy, Daddy, big sister, baby sister—move fitfully and fearfully into the future, into the hard lesson of how to become a family. In the spring of 1999 my husband and I buy a house in suburbia, twenty miles away. In-town real estate is beyond what we can pay, so we impulsively decide to buy a house where we can afford it. It is a beautiful brick house with a two-story foyer and a huge family room and soft, carpeted bedrooms upstairs. It has in-ground sprinkling systems and a garden tub in the master suite. It turns out to be all wrong.

I do not know how to talk to the other parents at the neighborhood pool. I do not dress like the other mothers or think like them or act like them. And I cannot pretend. I observe this community of mommies with my pensive gaze as if I am scrutinizing a species other than my own. Conversations about picking up the husband's shirts. Shared laments about his inability to cook anything beyond toast. Chatter about which beach resort provides the best vacation. I do not attend the scrapbooking parties to which I am invited. I cannot imagine sitting and cutting out pink spirals, orange spirals, while making conversation about potty training and sippy cups. I want to fit in more. Things would be easier. Instead, I write email and read poems and take hot baths in the garden tub. I play with my girls in the lovely backyard. I read to them and take photographs that I stack absent-mindedly in drawers and on shelves. *One of these days I have got to put these in albums,* I think to myself. But instead, I record other images as I sit here now, typing these words.

7 BLIND SPOT

2000. Every day I swallow the elliptical pill that keeps my sleep steady and my mood more or less okay. But something is still very wrong. It is something that lies deeper than seven hours of unbroken sleep, beyond the ability to grade forty tests or write a statement about my teaching. It is something that has come undone, some aspect of my being that has been neglected in its hiding, gone awry to some forgotten place.

It is the deep craving to tell this story.

It is the hunger to create some meaning.

To write of the dangerous edge I traveled during my starvation. Of the tearing of childbirth, and of its grace. Of the light filtering in through the birch trees and onto the pages of the book in my girl's hands. Of my lightness of being and of my heaviness of being. Paris and North Carolina and New Mexico and Georgia.

I did not talk with my father much while I was growing up. There was no language. I did not know the grammar of my longing to communicate and so I played my violin and studied my books. I moved drifts of snow when I was asked. I did not mow the lawn. That was too dangerous for a girl.

There were few conversations between just Dad and me. I remember one very clearly. 1983. He was teaching me to drive on the highway. He had already taught me automatic shift (on our massive orange and white Suburban) and stick shift (a tan Plymouth Horizon).

Now we were on the freeway in an early spring in northern Ohio. Heading up to Michigan, I believe. My father looked at my emaciated hands on the steering wheel. Piano-playing hands. Fingers that performed concertos and vibrato. Fingers that lifted forkfuls of food to my lips. Hands that conjugated French verbs in all tenses.

The high school ring that he had bought for me spun around my ring finger as I drove. He mentioned it. I said the ring was too big. He asked, "Isn't it because you've lost so much weight?" I deflected this possibility. Those passing moments composed the longest conversation he and I were to have about my anorexia. The Suburban continued to speed down the freeway, driven by a slender, sick girl seated next to her father.

It was time to change lanes. My father began to speak importantly, crucially, about the "blind spot." The blind spot, he explained, existed on either side of the car at all times. It was the place on either side where the driver's peripheral vision could not ascertain whether or not another car was right there, alongside her own vehicle. Even the side mirrors, angled just so, he explained, would not always perceive if a car was encroaching within the blind spot.

This was dangerous. If I did not check the blind spot before changing lanes, I could head swiftly into oblivion.

The blind spot must be seen, checked, verified. It was everywhere the possibility of loss and harm. To this day I still remember what my father taught me: never to trust the mirrors alone.

Reflection never tells the whole story. It is like the woman looking into the mirror of herself while giving birth. Better to go into the blind spot of each push, better not to peer into the reflection of the mystery taking place, the first separation, the birth of your child.

Sometimes I still become mystified by this blind spot. I might be about to change lanes, to the right or to the left. I look in a split second. My father was right—Oh, there is a car—Do not move—Do not trust the side mirrors. This could be a matter of life and death. In the back seat my two daughters laugh or fuss or drink juice or look at the trees.

The blind spot is the space I move into and out of. Where I suspect most of us live at times. The possibility of loss speeding up over our left or right shoulder. The inability to trust what a piece of glass purports to say. The encounter with destruction a split second in the making. Do not move either way—a car is coming, a big truck is coming, your father taught you this as your high school ring with the pink stone slid around your thin finger.

This is something never to be forgotten.

The urgency of his lesson.

The blind spot that beckons.

Its supreme importance as nonmeaning.

What he could not tell me when I was seventeen is that the blind spot follows you. It is not merely something to check and then avoid. It exists as opaque thought always near, over your left shoulder, over your right shoulder. Right there, here, where you cannot see it. You must turn and check, and as you do, you take the risk of not seeing what is in front of you. Past and future forgotten as you concentrate on the present strip of road.

Something in me wanted this collision with not seeing, with opaque thought, with a dark blankness that might swallow the tension between the present and all that is not present, with the possibility that exists outside of four tires on pavement or a loose ring around a finger. My father's warning came to me far too late. In my mind I was already driving into the place that I could not see. I had been heading toward it for a long time.

This writing is a going-in to that black—the ink on this page. The meaning of not knowing that gives sense to the strip of road in your thought. A longing too intense to sustain. Loving someone so much that you want to recoil. Watching your daughters play together, hold each other in their arms during a scary bit of cartoon.

Your six-year-old running toward the school building, her birdlike legs carrying her toward her desk and a story, the playground and the teacher's care. And you, standing there, watching her disappear behind the white door. Turning toward your car with its steering wheel, its four tires, the trunk that houses empty paper bags and stretched elastic cords, the spare tire you still have not learned to attach in the event of unforeseen crisis.

Spring 2000. The blind spot is starting to circle closer toward me, erasing the view of my life that offers me a window through which to see. I am losing my way. And I want to. The dark blankness is fascinating, of course—it is what we *want and need* to watch for. This is what my father neglected to tell me (how could he?)—that the opacity beckons. A way out and over, through and beyond.

Suburbia. I am blind to what is not right about it. I cannot talk with the other parents. I do not fit in. I cannot bear to face it. I do not care about tending to my lawn, I do not care about home entertaining, gardening, the neighborhood newsletter that circulates from house to house. Its cheerful news and careful directions for leaf disposal and covered dish events.

I go to collect the mail. October 1999. In the oblong metal box with the folding flag on one side is a certified letter. Emory Postpartum Mood Disorders Clinic. Certified. So that they will be sure I have received it. I am not allowed to come back. My treatment for postpartum depression has been terminated. I have failed to "comply." I "must" show greater "compliance" with the conditions for my treatment.

I finish reading the letter and then I look up. The neighbor's toy-sized dog looks up at me. I meet its gray gaze with complete indifference. The blue milligrams of Zoloft in my bloodstream dissolve and move through my bloodstream. I do not know where I am going to fill my prescription. Hmmm. This is bad. My thoughts move into a rigid pane of glass, a blind spot of emptiness. I flip through the rest of the mail. There are discounts and special prices advertised everywhere. Opportunities that may not last beyond this weekend. Lots of color and numbers. Baby Madeleine needs to be picked up from her toddler program soon. I will need to attach my seatbelt, get on the freeway, watch for the blind spot because it could kill me.

This lack of seeing is an end, it is memory that you see before you even as it slips away, that shimmer of heat ahead of you on the highway. It is the dark continent of your body, the child that you do not see even as you push her out of you. It is her new form and the breaking down of your own. It is the blank, black space of what you want to say but cannot, what you should have said but did not, what you try to write or read now in the spaces of these words. It is that part of your father's gaze that you will never see because, as he has always told you, he is legally blind in that eye. It is the blue mood suspended at the edge of your mind.

It is the possibility of error and destruction. The certified letter you have just received in the mail. The toy-sized dog looking up at you while you stand alone at the end of a curved driveway in a place that is all wrong. It is the shadow of your own absence, your own reduction, unknown shapes of thought that might overtake to collide.

I call my psychiatrist at Emory. He explains that there is an attendance policy for treatment. Three absences and you are out. Three strikes, then the certified letter. I have absolutely no recollection of being told this. I have missed three appointments over the space of six or seven months. The brief treatment at age nineteen, the year of talking to the therapist who left (me) to have her first child, a daughter, these fragments of unfinished therapy for twenty years of disordered eating are coming together in this telephone conversation, now, as I hold the document in my left hand.

I tell my psychiatrist that I cannot recall being informed of this attendance policy. I explain that at the initiation of treatment I could not even concentrate on simple tasks at work, that poor concentration and broken thought are symptomatic of clinical depression. The symptoms themselves preclude the ability to focus, to concentrate, to retain. My voice breaks into one light sob. He tells me that "this happens all the time." Then he utters a few referrals. I scrawl them onto the back of the envelope containing my dismissal from his care.

Is it fall, or is it winter? Am I still on my sabbatical leave, or am I back in the classroom? I cannot put the pieces together, the speed and the changing lanes of remembrance. Late afternoon. Waiting for my husband. I drink two large glasses of white wine on a completely empty stomach. He comes home. We prepare the girls to go out for pizza. We drive past the square brick homes of our suburban neighborhood. Some families have packed away their fall flags and signs, the cheerful pumpkins and scarecrows. In their place have appeared Santas and fake red foil gifts that sit outside in the warm Georgia evening. I am totally lost. All I know is the scent of my children's soft skin and the way their hair swirls on their pillows as they sleep.

Halfway into the meal I lose consciousness. Alcohol hitting the empty cave of my stomach. Blackout. Blind spot. Mother of two, I still do not know how to nurture myself. Shame. Still fighting what had been left untreated nearly twenty years before.

Home. Back through the complacent streets with the artificial gifts placed neatly on the front stoops. Bed. My husband is angry. My thoughts fold in toward their own self-destruction, the nothingness of sleep.

Now I am turning to look at that darkness, the possibility that is always a split second away. In this writing. Shadow of remembered thought. Blacking out. Not waking up.

I pull out the strength to take care of myself. I know I need to find someone to continue treating me. And I cannot go back to Emory because of the three missed appointments over the space of seven months. Seven months that entailed a major professional review, caring for an infant, moving, commuting, teaching, putting soup cans away neatly in rows, deciding that I could not place placards with pumpkins on the front lawn.

I call one of the referrals and speak with the receptionist. After a few sentences of description, she says, "Oh, you take medication. You'll need to see our psychiatrist." "Yes," I say. I take down the directions.

It has been only twenty-four hours since I blacked out in public. Anger. Shame. I am broken and imperfect. I do not know how to eat. I cannot let myself eat. I can take care of others but not myself. My husband returns home. I kiss our beautiful girls. They are eating macaroni and cheese.

I drive through the decorated neighborhood. Icicle lights. Nets of tiny lighting placed gingerly over trimmed hedges. I am wearing old glasses, no makeup, a gray loose floral dress, brown clogs with socks. I pull out onto the highway. Atlanta is such a spread-out city. All sprawl. I crave the close quarters of Paris, New York, their seductions of scent and color and form. I speed down the highway, west and then north. I get lost. My thinking is swirled and indefinite. The depression is gaining on me. The faster I drive, the more I feel its fingers gripping my neck.

I am lost and I am late. The psychiatrist made room for me at 5:30. Because it is early winter it is pitch dark outside. I do not yet have a cell phone. I stop at a pay phone. The quarter clinks into its slot. The receiver is filthy. The phone book on its shelf is curled and torn and attached to a steel wire. I call and say I'm lost, I'm on my way.

I find the address. I walk in and talk to an intensely quiet, composed, intelligent man with brown hair and transparent blue eyes. He asks me questions. I tell him about the night before, losing consciousness in public, and how I cannot eat, and how I cannot return to Emory because of an attendance policy that I swear I do not remember, and he asks me how much I had to drink the night before, and I say two glasses of wine, and he writes notes and says, "They must have been pretty big glasses," and I say, "I guess so."

I tell him I am a French professor, a mother, a wife. Something about the lamplight in his office, his blue eyes, convinces me that I can try this once more, to get it right, to understand my body story, the ragged edge of my thoughts, the story and its blind spot that had gone unheard for fifteen years, through the lightness of the wedding body and the starving body, the heaviness of the maternal body, nearer to speaking this story, toward you reading these words.

The failed therapy, my torn body giving birth, the body I am still learning to feed, the curves I am still trying to let in, not to neglect their beauty any more, not to fear my own softness, the sound of my own voice, the shape of what I write.

The virgin birches and the lilacs of my girl body. Its loss. The recuperation now, in this trace. The wings of a snow angel imprinted upon Ohio snow. The blades of ice skates. The copper ring given to me by a boy in fourth grade. The moment, not long after, when he asked for it back. Me pining after his copper hair and eyes for the next twelve years, barely summoning the courage even to speak.

The broomstick being shoved deep into that prisoner, that woman, while I watched in wild quiet fear, while snow fell outside and I tried to lean against my mother's warmth.

The white dresses. The tea-length dress with the blue satin sash. The boy on top of me, as I fight him off. The wedding dress in which I inhabited a moment's dream of transparency, without the shadow of thought's edge or shape, my strong groom at my side then and now.

The white reduction of bone that defined my body story, its restraint, its remote language, the anger that it cannot say. My body as hiding place. Angel of sharp angles, silent, removed. Studying French and playing violin. A dress with tulle that floats above the bone while I let another boy take me into his broad arms.

Studying. Riding my bike. Leaving America. Going into the seduction of French. Finding the strength. Discovering the color of oils, the curves of statues. Speaking Italian. Reading English poets. Being in love.

The cloister of my heart, of my blank origin. Bluest shadow on snow. New Mexico with its wild violet light. Giving birth. Feeling that heat, that tremendous release. My body laid bare. Nursing. Silver milk. Torn blood.

Work. Atlanta. City unknown. Teaching. Starving again. Paris with its gargoyles and spires, its golds and its catacombs of bones. Paris the place of my becoming, French the place where this story begins to be told.

Giving birth again. My flower opening up. Tiny toes, a mouth circling for milk. My body unsettling. My thoughts racing ahead of my shadow, self-hatred, falling in love with my child.

All of these experiences had led me into the blind spot of driving through the night, looking for this man. The Midwestern cold, pink and white southern blooms, Paris in delicious abandon, the place in my mind that cast no shadow because no light could get in.

The story of talking to this man, this quiet and brilliant psychiatrist, is the story of preparing to write these words. It is the awakening to the blind desire to write. It is his walking alongside me into that place in my mind.

Learning to accept the softness of my voice, soft curves of my body. Learning how to put food into my mouth without fear. Talking about the fear of loss that follows me around in my thoughts every day. The losses I recall and the ones I do not. My mother's mother being lowered into the earth when I was thirteen, my father's mother, dust, being lowered into the earth when I was thirteen. The brokenness of my grandparents' bodies. A grandmother in a wheelchair and a grandfather with a cane. Illness and bravery. A grandfather who was injured when a boiler exploded.

Guilt and shame. I have been given things I do not deserve. Paris and French. A tall, graceful body. The desire and the ability to write this story.

The need to stop hiding. To laugh with my two girls. Writing as a release from hiding. Speaking as a release from restriction.

This man is going to sit with me, in the blind space, in the box of glass, and listen to me speak of all these things. I am going to lie in the quiet of his office, in quiet lamplight. I am going to cry more than I ever could have foreseen. I am going to get worse before I get better. I black out one more time, the same story, white wine poured into the empty cave of my stomach. Compulsion to repeat. There are going to be entire sessions when all I do is cry. And he patiently sits with me, the patient, the professor, the mother, the writer of this story.

How was it that this doctor, at this time, began to make a difference? I cannot be absolutely certain. I know that my fearsome responsibility to my daughters required me to get out of that blind spot. I know that I had been waiting for twenty years to make sense of my experience, to move the pieces of the puzzle into some order. I know that he was—and still remains—committed to providing me with a full and complete treatment. He wants this for me even when I try mightily to resist it. Even when I insist that I do not deserve it.

In one of his famous essays, the sixteenth-century writer Michel de Montaigne examines one of the most intense relationships of his life—his friendship with Etienne de La Boétie. He ponders the mystery of their mutual recognition. Why the two of them, he asks himself? And then he writes «parce que c'était lui, parce que c'était moi»: "because it was him, because it was me." Montaigne does not intend here to be coy. He is simply explaining the red edge and opaque center of love.

Neither fate nor destiny; rather, a stroke of good luck, my initial consultation with this psychiatrist who was in the final stages of his psychoanalytic training. My work allowed me a certain flexibility of time. The fee was manageable.

In the past—at college, and in the years following my move to Atlanta—my repeated efforts at treatment were cut short by the limited quantity imposed by policy or HMOs. Each time I would begin to put the puzzle together, there would be an end and I would lose the therapy. This time, I was extremely fortunate.

Change and growth have come through a long, slow process of representation. It is an ongoing process. Most often it feels like two steps forward, one step back. The cure is never something to be understood in a single moment. It always makes itself known imperfectly.

Representation in language has helped me even more than antidepressant medication. Putting words together in some coherent way, making them communicate what I have experienced. This process is not unlike a child's building structures with blocks.

Psychoanalytic treatment has allowed me to speak my way out of that sharp box of glass, out of the blind spot. It often feels like the psychological equivalent of learning to walk. Constantly stumbling and then picking myself up.

In psychoanalysis, the tool of the slow, imperfect cure is language. This tool holds the writer intimately within a duet of writing and speech.

The story of my speech in analysis has nurtured this writing. It is like tributaries that lead to rivers emptying into a wide sea. I have journals full of my scribblings from sessions with my doctor. A maze of circling dreams, the puzzle of speech in which I often get stuck. Writing every which way, arrows pointing everywhere. A lot of words scratched out in crosshatched ink. Slowly the journals began to take the form of the book you are holding in your hands.

I am slowly going to begin to eat lunch. I am going to gain a little weight. I am no longer going to lose my way on purpose. Trial and error. But I am always going to be turning to check for the blind spot. Not out of fear. Rather, out of interest. The ink that forms these words, the pupil of the eye, my daughters' cheeks.

Nearly twenty years of place, of reduction to bone and swelling to fruit, of opening and of closing, of moving in space and moving in time.

Leaving that suburb. Moving back into Decatur. Back in boxes. Stepping out of the box of glass in which I had hidden.

Driving so often to his office that I know every light by heart. Writing this book in the space of five months. The fretfulness and the restlessness. Acceptance of a certain instability. The reflection in the mirror that never truly knows. The truth in my children's bodies, music of their forms. Swallowing the blue elliptical pill every day. Swinging open the gate of this writing and allowing myself to walk within. Listening to the sound of my fingers flying over these keys—innocent as birches, lilacs, drifts of snow.

I was ready to do just about anything not to face the fear and uncertainty of writing this story, the risk of entering into its presence of meaning and its absence of light.

> The cost of resistance was great. The price of embracing this
> 	risk is great, too.
> What I have been seeking here can be found only in the
> 	unrequited realm of writing.
> Something out of time.
> Writing as an out-of-body experience, space of freedom.
> Gardens of unseen form that might be felt but may never be
> 	seen,
> remembered but never fully retold,
> like the separation of birth, the communion of loss,
> the adieu that I record in this moment, within this page
> that speaks the end of your gift of reading this now.

READING GUIDE

Body Story

by Julia K. De Pree

A note from the author:

Dear Readers,

This guide is intended to assist reading groups in discussion and interpretation of *Body Story*. Organized according to the chapters in the book, the guide also includes creative writing activities for groups who are interested. The creative writing activities are to be done individually. Writers can share their creative work during group discussions—perhaps before or after the chapter questions. If your group feels more courageous, you might consider compiling your creative writing responses as a group scrapbook or printing them together in a booklet or posting them on a Web site. Let the writing take you somewhere new.

Thank you so much for your interest in my work. I would be happy to correspond with group participants and individual writers. You may e-mail me by going to my Web site: http://juliadepree.agnesscott.edu

Suggested group size: six to eight people

Suggested discussion time: three or four discussion sessions, forty-five to sixty minutes for each session

Preliminary Group Discussion

1. What were your thoughts when you first looked at the cover? What are your impressions of the cover art? Does the cover art make you think of anything specific from your own background?
2. What are your impressions of the title of the book? The book is nonfiction, but the author has used the word "story" in the title. What comes to mind when you think of storytelling and stories? Does the title imply fiction? Discuss the possible intention here.

Chapter 1: Body Story

Individual creative writing option:

Free writing: Write whatever comes to mind on the topic of your own body. Don't judge yourself as you write; just allow your thoughts to go onto the page. If you don't like what you have written, you can tear it up later! Write as much or as little as you like, whether it is one sentence or many pages. Complete sentences are not necessary.

Now read what you have written. What do you think of it? Don't judge yourself too harshly. Consider editing your work for the next group meeting. You might consider reading just a few sentences, or one or two paragraphs.

Group discussion:

1. What is the prevailing metaphor on page 1 of the book? In other words, what is the main image that seems to be informing the writing?
2. Choose two or three sentences from this chapter that

caught your attention for whatever reason, whether because (1) you admired them, or (2) you did not admire
them, or (3) you did not understand them. Did any
other members of the group choose any of the same
sentences?

3. Does the writing in chapter 1 seem to you predomi-
nately concrete or abstract? Why?

Chapter 2: Girl Body

Group discussion:

1. Notice the shifts in time in this chapter. Where do they
occur in the chapter? What is their effect on the reader's
perception and understanding of the content?

2. Consider the question on page 14: "Was it not wonderful
to know the answers to your body's questions, before the
doubt set in?" Is the question clear to you, or unclear?
How would you answer the question?

3. The chapter ends with a depiction of a disturbing
memory. The author recounts her experience of view-
ing a televised representation of rape as a child. How
did you react to this passage? What is the possible purpose of this passage in terms of the overall narrative?

Chapter 3: Virgin Body

Individual creative writing option:

On a clean sheet of paper, write what comes to mind when
you think of the word "virginity." Write as much as you want.
Then consider what you wrote down. Are you surprised by
it? Now, save it, tear it up, or bring it to group discussion.

Group discussion:

1. Have you read many literary texts that depict individuals'
memories of virginity? How many authors or texts can
you list?

2. Did you identify with the author's experience in this chapter? If so, what allowed you to identify with her personal experience? If not, what prevented you from identifying with her?

3. Was there one moment in this chapter that really caught your attention? If so, why?

Chapter 4: Starving Body

Group discussion:

1. This chapter is longer than the previous chapters. Do you think there is any reason for that?

2. De Pree does not explain the exact reasons she developed anorexia nervosa. Can you suggest why she avoids discussing this? What elements seem to have contributed to her developing the affliction?

3. Do you have a close relationship with anyone who has had an eating disorder? If so, in what ways are De Pree's descriptions of her experience in this chapter similar to that person's experience?

4. What surprises you in this chapter? What annoys you? Does anything in this chapter confuse you? Does anything in this chapter frighten you?

5. What kinds of images seem to inform De Pree's writing at this point in the book? Is there a pattern to these images?

6. What is the role of music and literature in this part of the book?

Chapter 5: Wedding Body

Individual creative writing option:

If you are (or used to be) married, think back to your wedding day. Now write down whatever comes to mind. Complete sentences are not necessary. If you have a wedding photo nearby as you write, you may want to look at the picture for a few moments and then write. Alternatively, write down some of your thoughts and feelings about a bride's wedding gown. How would you articulate the nonverbal meaning of the bridal gown? Write a list of words or write in sentences. Now, save it, tear it up, or bring it to group discussion.

Group discussion:

1. In what ways does De Pree relay a sense of detachment from her own wedding preparations? How does she explain this detachment?
2. What does the imagery of the wedding gown communicate to the reader?
3. Why do you think that the author emphasizes the visual aspects of her experience as a bride? Do you agree that the meaning of the bride and of her gown is primarily visual? Do you agree that this meaning is somewhat illusory?
4. At the end of this chapter, De Pree shifts her narration to the present and describes a moment in the process of writing the book. In this passage she mentions the "tension . . . between futility and grace" (70). How do you interpret that phrase?

Chapter 6: Giving Birth

Group discussion:

1. Throughout the book, De Pree's body story is also a story of geographical place: living in a physical body and being grounded in a specific physical place provoke pleasure as well as sorrow. Discuss this parallel as it evolves in chapter 6.
2. In what ways does De Pree's professional progress contrast with her personal and family life in this chapter?
3. The author writes that she was initially reluctant to get pregnant for the first time. Does she explain why? To what might you attribute her reluctance?
4. Discuss your reactions to the depiction of the author's first experience of giving birth, in New Mexico. What details caught your attention?

5. Did you react differently to the second depiction of childbirth in this chapter?

6. How are medical professionals and the experience of hospitalization depicted in this chapter? Are they represented positively, negatively, or both?

Chapter 7: Blind Spot

Individual creative writing option:

Preferably before reading the chapter, write down whatever comes to mind when you consider the phrase "blind spot." Taking what you have written as a point of departure, structure a poem, a story, a letter, or any other kind of creative text. Share your writing with other members of your reading group if you wish.

Group discussion:

1. This chapter begins with a memory of the author and her father. How would you describe their interactions? What does this scene add to the story overall?

2. Throughout the book, the author documents her interactions with various medical providers: nurses, therapists, midwives, and her psychiatrist. Do you feel that, overall, the medical community is depicted favorably in the book?

3. The final pages of the book revisit all the dominant memories and experiences that have preceded them. How did you react to the final pages?

4. *Body Story* spans more than three decades of the author's life. Do you sense that the essence of her personality is the same at the end of her story? If so, how would you describe that essence? If not, in what way does she seem fundamentally changed?